FAITH

ITS NATURE AND ITS WORK

Handley Dunelm.

FAITH

ITS NATURE AND ITS WORK

BY

HANDLEY C. G. MOULE, D.D.
Bishop of Durham
Author of "Thoughts for the Sundays of the Year," etc., etc.

Wipf and Stock Publishers
199 W 8th Ave, Suite 3
Eugene, OR 97401

Faith
Its Nature and Its Work
By Moule, Handley C.G.
ISBN 13: 978-1-55635-254-6
ISBN 10: 1-55635-254-9
Publication date 2/5/2007
Previously published by Cassell, 1909

TO THE DEAR AND INSPIRING MEMORY

OF MY BROTHER AND FRIEND,

JOHN BARTON,

WHO, HAVING THROUGH

FAITH WROUGHT RIGHTEOUSNESS,

FELL ASLEEP,

NOVEMBER 26, 1908

PREFACE

THE aim of this little book is modest. It makes no pretension to deal with its momentous subject-matter in a fashion either scientific or exhaustive. To be suggestive of further enquiry and reflection is one of its chief purposes, and to be practical is its chief purpose of all.

It approaches Faith, for study and discussion, from the avowedly Christian point of view. In Faith we have one of the great watchwords of Christianity; indeed, its greatest watchword in a certain sense, great with an importance vital and practical, bearing always on the most exacting problems of real life. Faith deals with the eternal and transcendent. But it does so in order that the man of Faith may deal aright, in the spirit befitting the man of God, with the seen, the felt, the temporal, the present, with the real exigencies of conscience and the heart, with the actual pressure of difficulty upon thought and will, with the sorrows and the joys of life, with the call to act *on earth* under the influence of Heaven.

All through these pages our enquiries will be guided and assisted by the Holy Scriptures, the Book of Light placed by our Master in the hand of Faith. Something will be said in the course of the work upon the reasons, or rather upon some of the reasons, for our reliance upon the Bible as the Oracle of God, as Faith's "lamp unto the feet and light unto the path." But from the first it will be taken for granted that we approach and pursue our theme as Christians, and therefore with a reverential regard for that Book, manifold yet one, which comes to the Christian solemnly commended by his Lord; the Written Word, endorsed, informed, inspired, by the Living Word Himself.

HANDLEY DUNELM.

February, 1909.

CONTENTS

FAITH . . .
THE WORD . .
AND THE THING

B

FAITH

CHAPTER I

FAITH: THE WORD AND THE THING

THE word FAITH is old in our language. As long ago as the thirteenth century, in the days of Edward I., in a poem called "Havelok the Dane," we find it in the form "feyth." It is close akin to the Latin *fides,* the root of our word fidelity. *Fides* again goes back for its ancestry to the vast antiquity of the Sanskrit language, the Asiatic mother of Greek, and Latin, and German, and English, not to speak of other members of the large Aryan family. In Sanskrit is found a word whose form and sound are closely akin to *fides,* and the meaning of that Sanskrit word is "to bind."

Already here we have a suggestion as to some sides of the meaning of this brief but pregnant word, Faith. For Faith connects itself with thoughts which have everything to do with close relations, with living links, with the trust which grasps and the truth which is grasped, with union between the spirit which exercises Faith and the Object to which in Faith that spirit clings.

Passing now from the ancestry of the word Faith to its meaning and usage, we note first that the word lends itself in our common speech to two references, answering significantly one to another. We may call one the passive and the other the active sense of Faith. The passive sense is seen where the word denotes the quality or character which invites trust—trustworthiness, fidelity. So we speak familiarly of a man's "good faith," in the sense of his honesty of purpose; and thus the poet sings, in a memorable lyric, how

> "Kind hearts are more than coronets,
> And simple faith than Norman blood."

The active sense of the word is seen where it denotes the confidence, the reliance, which goes out towards the trusted thing or person, and rests on it, and lays hold of it. So we speak of a soldier's faith in his trusted captain, a patient's faith in his trusted physician, the faith of a school or a party in a trusted leader of thought or of action. The two senses are closely and interestingly connected with each other, for truth invites trust, and trust has a great capacity to develope truth in the sense of fidelity. But they are obviously senses which can be, and often must be, distinguished from each other.

The passive sense of Faith is, as a fact,

much less commonly used than the other. For once that we speak of Faith in the sense of truthfulness or trustworthiness we speak of it many times in the sense of confidence, reliance, trust. Accordingly, Faith must be looked at almost always from the active side. We must mainly think of it, in matters of religion, for example, as it stands connected with such thoughts as that of the outgoing of the human spirit towards the unseen and eternal in confidence, reliance, trust.

We observe here, first, how extremely familiar the word Faith is, taken in this sense, in our common speech of every day. As we recollected just now, we use freely and constantly such expressions as faith in a principle, faith in an enterprise, faith in a remedy, faith in a person—in a teacher, perhaps, or leader, or doctor, or lawyer, or friend. With equal naturalness we use the word Faith with reference to a guide of our bodies up a difficult mountain, or through a dangerous illness, and to a guide of our minds through their problems on the way to a satisfying answer. To the word Faith so used one dominant notion always attaches, namely, confidence, reliance, trust.

Let us think a little further over this obvious fact of common English diction. We are approaching the study of sacred truths, and of religious language as used for the expression of them. Then all the more we ought first to think of this word Faith, so largely used in reference to things divine, as it is used in reference to the simplest things of the ordinary day. For there is no great religious word used in spiritual connexions in the Holy Scriptures which is not best studied first in the light of its non-religious use. Our Lord and His Apostles never gave an *un*-natural meaning to a word, however much they applied it to *super*-natural matters. Would we think clearly and safely, then, about Faith in God? Let us first, as one preliminary, think over what we mean by Faith in man.

Taking the word thus into "the light of common day," let it suggest to us naturally some such remarks as the following.

i. Faith is not precisely identical with belief, persuasion, conviction. We do not naturally use it in so wide a reference as that of these other words. For example, an English soldier at Waterloo would probably have a full belief, persuasion, and conviction, as to the eminent military skill and mighty leadership of both the opposing chiefs. But he would use the word Faith of only Wellington. In the greatness of Bonaparte he would see only danger. In that of Wellington he would see an object for his confidence. And he would express, or at least he would feel, a boundless faith in Wellington accordingly.

ii. A further thought rises out of this. We see that the word Faith is what we may call a word of good omen. It connects itself naturally and by a law of mental association with what is friendly and beneficial. In religion accordingly it has a true and beautiful affinity with the benignant promises of God, with His gracious purposes and actions, or, better still, with HIM the all-benignant, all-gracious, all-trustworthy Promiser and Giver. Faith is trust going out to truth, and to truth not anywise considered but presented to us in mercy, in love; truth as the manifestation of the will of Him who is Love, who is in particular full of (Titus iii. 4) "kindness and love towards man."

iii. These last words suggest a further thought over our common use of the word Faith. It is the nature and tendency of the word to go out towards a person. We may have belief or conviction regarding the most abstract idea possible. But when we speak of having Faith we habitually direct the notion either towards a veritable person, or towards something which we personify in the mind. Even when we speak of Faith in a medicine, or of Faith in a political principle, or in a maxim of business, I venture to say that we suggest to our minds, however dimly, a picture in which the remedy or the principle, or the maxim, seems to take life and action, and to come forth personally to guide and help us. I do not attempt to explain the fact, as fact I think it is. Perhaps we may trace in it a far-off echo of that primeval Sanskrit word whose meaning is "to bind," and which suggests a living link between the Faith and the thing in which the Faith rests. However, I repeat my belief that the natural, and therefore the religious, tendency of the word Faith is to find its response and its repose in a person. It is an attitude of personal reliance upon personal capacity and fidelity.

iv. Yet another reflection arises from our everyday use of the word Faith. The word connects itself naturally not with mere thought but with action. It is essentially practical. When we speak for example of Faith in a general, or Faith in a physician, we do not merely signify our full persuasion that they are skilled, and competent, and friendly to us. We imply that we either actually confide in their skill and power for our benefit, or that we are ready to do so when the need comes. Faith is trust which either actually *en*trusts, or is ready to do so. In fact, as we said at the outset, Faith (except in its rarer passive sense of fidelity) is essentially active. It goes out to its object. It acts, or at least it is ready at need to act, on its view of its object. It obeys the leader, or is ready to obey him, because in the battle, or on the march, it trusts him. It lies resolutely quiet under the painful treatment of the doctor, it positively submits to him, it makes a practical surrender to him, or at least it is prepared to do so when the hour comes—because it trusts him.

Faith is as broadly distinguished as possible from Work, in some great aspects of that word. Yet Faith, in the light of what we have just said, is nothing if not "workful"; it is pregnant of practical results.

v. The familiar use of the word Faith

outside religion reminds us further that it is always, in an important sense, the antithesis to Sight. It always indicates an element of the unseen and unknown somewhere in the matter. No doubt Faith and Sight stand in a close connexion with each other, and often seem to run over, so to speak, into one another. Faith, in its true and sane sense, cannot live without some foothold on what we may call sight. But Faith *in itself* is precisely that which ventures out beyond sight, and moves and works in the dark, in the unseen, in the unknown.

Take for illustration the case of the physician, to which we alluded just now. You are ill, and you send for your doctor, and you give yourself over to his care, because you have Faith in him. What does it mean? Your physician is quite visible to your eyes, and his treatment is felt by your body; all this falls under the heading of sight. But your Faith in him is that attitude of thought and will which leaps off into what to you is the unknown region of his medical science and training. He knows what you do not know about your disease, and about the proper remedies or reliefs. You know him well enough, as a man, to trust him out of sight, so to speak, with things which you know not but which he knows. Precisely in that region, in what is a dark void to your own understanding, your Faith in your physician lives, and moves, and works.

So again with the military leader. A story is told of two English soldiers in the South African War of 1899-1902. They were toiling through the night, over the trackless veld, on one of Lord Roberts's great strategic marches. "What is the use of it?" said one of the two, well-nigh worn out, stumbling on in the twilight over the rough and endless plain. "Never mind," said the other; "come along; Roberts knows." This was precisely Faith. Its foothold was firmly set on the man's experience of his chief's capacity and power. From that foothold it reached boldly out into the unknown, and trusted the chief's hidden plan without a murmur. The unknown is Faith's natural atmosphere.

vi. Yet a further reflection emerges here. It is that Faith, while thus, by its very nature, dealing with the unknown, seeing thus, as it were, in the dark, nevertheless is something quite different from a mysterious and independent faculty of intuition. Sometimes, in the religious sphere, we find Faith thus described, as if it denoted a power to penetrate things eternal and inscrutable in a fashion almost akin to "second sight." To illustrate this somewhat roughly, take the familiar phrase, "the ages of Faith." This is commonly used to denote periods when men's minds found no difficulty, or at least much less difficulty than most of us feel now, in conceiving of supernatural presences and actions all around them, in regarding earth and air as peopled with unseen beings, pagan gods of the forest, fairies of the midnight field, or again glorified human saints appearing as helpers and deliverers in hours of need. The word Faith in such a connexion is used as if it meant a capacity or receptivity for realization of the impalpable and invisible, a mysterious power of insight, piercing beyond the veil of sense.

I am far from denying that we are surrounded by invisible personal existences; indeed, I firmly believe that we are. And I am perfectly sure that some minds are much more awake than others with a mysterious consciousness that it is so. It seems clear that certain races of men are thus especially conscious of the unseen—the Celtic race, for example. But I should not give the term Faith to such special consciousness, or to the capacity for it. I should describe such a power rather as a sort of subtle *sense,* just as when (if I may illustrate my meaning thus) you find, as you do sometimes find, persons who can tell without sight or sound when you are near them, in a dark room, perhaps, or behind their backs. A peculiar consciousness of the unseen world is not Faith; it is a faculty of perception, liable like other faculties to wrong use as well as to right, to mistakes as well as to verity. But in any case it has the nature more of sensation than of Faith.

For Faith, let me repeat it, when we test the meaning by the use of every day, is essentially not sensation but an attitude or action of reliance. The soldier's faith in "Roberts" was no mysterious sensation of the general's reality, or of his nearness; it was a reliance on him in his unknown aim and movement, based on knowledge of the man.

It is not difficult to see how the use of the word Faith in such a phrase as "ages of Faith" connects itself with the proper use. If Faith, as we have seen, finds in the unknown and unseen its true sphere of action, it is easy to pass on to the thought that Faith means a power of seeing into the unknown and unseen, the faculty of the prophet, the seer, the inspired recipient of dream and vision. But such a transition is really a confusion of one thought with another.

Faith, when we test it by common use, and also, as I think, when we examine the word in Scripture as applied to things divine, is the attitude in which, while we are willing to leave the unseen as much unseen as ever, we yet *rely* on the action, or the promise, in the unseen, of One whom in some sense we know; taking it to be true and good, though it is altogether out of our sight, lying for the time beyond our every *sense*, bodily or spiritual.

It is not too much to say, in summing up these reflections, that, if we take common usage as our guide to the natural meaning of the great word Faith, we are safe in thinking that Faith means, on the whole, personal confidence, resting, ultimately at least, in a person or persons; confidence of the sort which is practical and active; which works in a way that passes beyond sight into the unseen and unknown; while yet it is not, in itself, any abnormal insight into the invisible. Rather, it leaves the invisible, in one respect, alone, in the sense that it relies, in that mysterious sphere, upon a will which it can absolutely trust—for it is the will of the God whom we know.

THE WORD FAITH IN SCRIPTURE

CHAPTER II

THE WORD FAITH IN SCRIPTURE

Thus far we have said very little about the Biblical use of the word Faith. This has been on purpose. I have already intimated my personal conviction that religious thought has suffered often from the assumption, more or less deliberately made, that because the great words of Religion have a supernatural application they have therefore in themselves, as words, a supernatural meaning, a meaning other than that which they bear in common life.

But surely it is not so. We may illustrate the point from a word yet more transcendently sacred in the Bible than Faith, even the word Love. Love appears in Scripture as a thing lifted to, or rather revealed from, the very sanctuary of Divine Being. "Love is of GOD." Yea, "GOD is Love." But that infinitely sacred reference of the word does not alter the natural meaning of the word in itself.

It has been finely said that Love is that which finds its felicity in another's good. If so, the word Love keeps its native meaning equally when it refers to the supreme and all-blessed Nature, which takes an eternal pleasure in the created being's purity and joy, and when it refers to the loyal Christian's heart, which finds its highest happiness in meeting the holy call of God that we should supremely love Him.

It is equally true to its natural meaning when it refers to the mutual kindness of Christians for one another, a "brotherly love" capable of sacrifices even unto death, and also when it refers to the loves and links of nature as God made it—the love of husband for wife, of mother for child, of friend for friend. We do not gain but lose by thinking of Love in relation to things divine and spiritual as a different term from Love in relation to things natural and human. We lose in distinctness, in simplicity, and in living warmth of thought. Even so it is with Faith.

But we now pass onwards and upwards to the actual use of the word Faith in that Book which is as supremely natural in one aspect as it is uniquely supernatural in another—the Bible. We shall think later of some of the reasons for our faith in the Bible, our personal reliance upon it as the organ of the revelation of our heavenly Father's mind and will. But we go to it now only to enquire into this particular matter in the vocabulary of the Bible—what, as a fact, is the Biblical use of the word Faith?

One phenomenon meets us here at once, and perhaps surprises us. In the Old Testament the word Faith hardly occurs at all. Taking the Authorized Version, we find it in only two isolated passages. The first is Deut. xxxii. 20: "Froward children, in whom is no Faith." The other is Hab. ii. 4: "The just shall live by his Faith." In both these places the Hebrew word is *emûnâh,* which tends to mean rather Faithfulness than Faith, or, to put it otherwise (*see page* 4), Faith passive rather than Faith active. But the fact remains that in the only two places in the Old Testament where we read "Faith" in the English Bible the trend of the word is towards trustworthiness rather than trust. And the Revised Version actually reads this into its margin in Habbakuk: "The just shall live in his faithfulness."

This phenomenon has many others to relieve it, so to speak. If *the word* Faith, in the trustful sense, is absent from Moses, and the Prophets, and the Psalms, *the thing* is abundantly there. From the grand example of Abraham's obedience, as he takes step after step in the dark, down to such minor yet most moving incidents as that of the widow of Zarephath, who trusted God's word against all appearances, Faith meets us everywhere.

When we come to study Heb. xi.* we shall see a long procession of the Old Testament saints pass before us, all of whom are instances of the victory of Faith. Again, other words are used in the Psalms and Prophets to convey essentially the same notion, particularly the word Hope.

* See Chapter xii.

Take for example Jer. xvii. 7, 17: "Blessed is the man whose hope the Lord is"; "Thou art my hope in the day of evil." * Obviously in both these cases the word Trust might take the place of Hope. As a fact, *the verb* "to trust" is used freely in the English Old Testament to represent Hebrew words more or less akin to the idea of "active Faith." In a few of these passages the Hebrew is closely connected with the noun (*emûnâh*) used in Hab. ii. 4, and interpreted by St. Paul as signifying Faith. Take for example Micah vii. 5: "*Trust* ye not in a friend."

A Concordance shows us at once that the Old Testament abounds in precepts, promises, and examples relating to the

* The Hebrew word rendered "hope" in verse 7 (*mibhtach*) is not the same as that so rendered in verse 17 (*machseh*). But both are fairly represented by it. The idea in both cases is a resource which invites the expectation of safety.

privilege and duty of reliance, under difficulties, in a faithful God. Yet the singular fact remains that the Hebrew mind developed no single word which, as a noun in common use, embodied that idea in the form of "current coin." And this fact surely has its mental and spiritual lesson.

The elder Dispensation did indeed cultivate in a wonderful way the faculty of reliance, and enjoined in many ways the exercise of it. Yet that side of the spiritual life was not its main matter. Rather, its function was to humble man and discipline him, with a view towards a future which was to be more free and glorious. Its watchwords, dominant and infinitely important, were man's sin, God's righteousness and holiness, worship, obedience, awe, law. Every one of these watchwords was to be wonderfully emphasized and deepened in the New Testament. But the New Testament was to place them all under the radiant light of a full and fully manifested Redemption; it was to illuminate them with the pure and gracious glory of Incarnation, Atonement, and Pentecost. For it therefore was reserved the large and liberal use of the noun Faith, in the sense of a simple but profound reliance upon Him who has so shewn His face in the light that it becomes the instinct and characteristic of His true worshippers to trust His will in the dark. The elder revelation led steadily up to this great end. But it was not yet the time to speak with perfect freedom and fulness of it. Truth rather than Trust, Fear rather than Faith, was the deepest and most characteristic message of the Word of God till "the fulness of the times was come."

It is significant in this connexion that

the Septuagint, "The Seventy," that is to say, the Greek-speaking Egyptian Jews who, before the Christian Era, translated the Hebrew Scriptures into Greek, rarely, if ever, use the word Faith (*pistis*) in any but the passive sense; that is to say, the word *pistis* represents with them not so much Trust as Truth, "good Faith."

Before their time, in the old "classical" Greek, the word *pistis* often bore the meaning Trust. But in the so-called "common" Greek, that phase of the language which was used by religious writers in Greek in the ages between the Prophets and the Apostles (because it was the phase used by everyone in their times and countries), *pistis* appears to have come to bear the sense of Trust only just in time to provide it as the needed and perfect term for the use of the Lord and His messengers through whom the world was at length to hear that Gospel whose inmost precept is, " Believe ! " *

Once arrived at the New Testament period, and scrutinizing the language of the Evangelists and Apostles, we find everywhere the word Faith, noun as well as verb. A good Concordance to the Greek Testament will shew the noun Faith (*pistis*) occurring more than 230 times, and the related verb (*pisteuein*) about 250 times. Manifestly, the idea which these words denote had risen into a new and wonderful prominence and importance since the Old Testament periods. To a degree unprecedented, and in a way full of significance, Faith had become the watchword of the message from the Heavens.

Looking now more closely into the

* See for much admirable matter on this subject Bishop Lightfoot's *Galatians*, Detached Note (2) after Chapter iii.

facts, and asking what side, aspect, or type of Faith is mainly in view in the Christian Scriptures, we find no difficulty in the answer. In the very great majority of cases Faith there means active Faith, the trust, the reliance, of the soul. There are exceptions, which we will consider in the next chapter. But the rule is large and impressive, and we may take a view of it at once.

For clearness, let us confine our view to the noun Faith (*pistis*). The use of the corresponding verb, *pisteuein*, needs little if any separate examination.*

* Unfortunately our language gives us no verb akin in derivation to the noun Faith, such a verb, for example, as "to *befaith*" would be. "*To believe*" is, of course, a good rendering of *pisteuein*, but its different root and shape prevent it from suggesting by itself the sameness of the thought denoted by it and by the noun Faith—a sameness which *pistis* and *pisteuein* make clear in Greek. See also the remarks above, *p.* 8 on a difference often found in the use of "Faith" and "Belief."—"Belief," "Believe," are connected in origin with roots denoting "love," "value."

Take then first some examples of the use of the word Faith by our Lord Himself:

"I have not found so great Faith, no, not in Israel" (Matt. viii. 10); "Thy Faith hath saved thee" (Matt. ix. 22); "O woman, great is thy Faith" (Matt. xv. 28); "Have Faith in God" (Mark xi. 22); "Where is your Faith?" (Luke viii. 25). We may add, although the Greek word in these places is a compound, of which *pistis* is only part: "Why are ye fearful, O ye of little Faith?" (Matt. viii. 26); "O thou of little Faith, wherefore didst thou doubt?" (Matt. xiv. 31).

Here, beyond all reasonable question, in the light of the context and circumstances of each utterance, we find the Lord using Faith in the sense of personal reliance. The Roman officer, the Galilean woman who touched the hem of the garment, the Syrophenician mother—each is welcomed and praised on the ground of a simple and unquestioning reliance on the will and power of the healing Christ. The disciples are reproved for their defect in such reliance; they have suffered themselves to be bewildered by difficulty or danger so that their hearts misgive them, and they tremble where they should have trusted.

The noun Faith (*pistis*), remarkably enough, not once occurs in the Fourth Gospel. But this defect in respect of the noun is abundantly made up for by the frequency of the verb (*pisteuein*). This occurs in the Gospel almost exactly one hundred times, and of these cases the very large majority give us the word from the lips of the Lord Himself.

We have the verb used with some important varieties of grammatical construction. Frequently it stands detached, as in John i. 7: "That all through him might believe." Frequently it appears in the phrase, "to believe *in*" (or more literally, "*into*") "the name of the Son of God"; or, again, "*upon* His name"; more simply still, "to believe *on*" (or literally, "*into*") "Him." Again we have it used where quite obviously the verb "to trust" rightly represents *pisteuein*, and is so used in the Revised Version. So, for instance: "Jesus did not trust Himself to them" (ii. 24); "If you trust not Moses' writings, how shall you trust My words?" (v. 47).

It is not too much to say that our Lord, as reported by the Evangelists, is found to use the Greek equivalents for Faith, the noun *pistis* and the verb *pisteuein*, invariably in the sense of confidence, reliance, trust, and the corresponding verbs. At least this is certain, that when we translate by such English words the Greek words as He uses them we get invariably a meaning which fits exactly into the context of His sayings and doings on each occasion, and it would be most difficult, to say the least, to find any other English word of which this would be true.

It is transparent then that upon an attitude of reliance He laid the utmost stress. Now by precept, now by parable, now by the discipline of circumstance, He commended that attitude to His followers as all-pleasing to Himself and all-helpful to their highest good. There was nothing which more delighted Him than to see that attitude taken by the human hearts that turned to Him for the succour of His power, for the bliss and rest of His lovingkindness. If ever anything like an abnormal exercise of Faith was visible to His gracious eyes He met it not only with complacency but with a *wondering* pleasure unspeakably moving as we see it in Him. Whatever the reason, such was the fact; to the Lord Jesus there was in the Faith of a human suppliant something which He met with a vivid pleasure and to which his response, at once or after a brief discipline of delay, was always generously large.

Did His Apostles after Him so emphasize the preciousness of Faith, in that sense, that it became the watchword of Christianity? They only trod in their Divine Master's track.

THE WORD FAITH IN SCRIPTURE .

CHAPTER III

THE WORD FAITH IN SCRIPTURE (*continued*)

We have examined, in the light of some typical and leading passages, our Lord's use of the great word Faith. We have seen Him taking it invariably in the sense of trust—trust in Himself, in His Father, in His Father's word, in His own "name." Now we pass on to the use of the word by the Apostles and Prophets to whom in the providence of God the writing of the Acts, Epistles, and Apocalypse was committed.

Taking any adequate Greek Concordance, or any carefully arranged English Concordance as the next best instrument of enquiry, we shall soon see some leading results emerge. Broadly speaking, we shall find that not invariably yet habitually the meaning of Faith with the New Testament writers is what is always its meaning with their Lord. Very much more often than not, where we find them using the words in question, particularly *pistis* and *pisteuein,* it is obvious that they use them in the sense of confidence, reliance, trust, while we also have a fairly large number of passages where other though kindred meanings of *pistis* are in place. Of these the most numerous and the most important are those which lead us to render *pistis* by some such word as Creed, finding it to denote, in the light of the connexion, not the attitude of trust but the summary and expression of the truths and facts on which the trust reposes—in other words, Creed.

On Creeds we shall speak in the next chapter. But it will be fitting here to dwell a little on one leading and remarkable passage of the New Testament, where not only does Faith mean Creed rather than reliance, but where it is all-important to a right understanding of Christian truth that we should see that it does so. That passage is the paragraph in St. James' Epistle (ii. 14–26), in which he discusses the relation between Faith and works, and decides that Faith without works cannot save the soul; yes, that Faith without works is dead.

The passage is of the highest interest in itself. If it stood alone in the New Testament it would always be noteworthy, as pressing home one of the gravest facts of the religious life, the urgent call to a practical and not only theoretical concurrence with the will of God. But an interest altogether peculiar attaches to it because of its acute apparent contrast in terms to some outstanding passages in the teaching of St.

Paul. St. James, in the most explicit language, tells us that "by works a man is justified, and not by Faith only." Equally explicitly we hear from St. Paul (Rom. iii. 28) "that a man is justified by Faith without the works of the law." And he follows up the words very shortly afterwards by bringing in as an illustration that very Abraham (Rom. iv. 1–22), whom St. James also cites to us—but as a witness on what seems to be the side exactly opposite.

The problem thus raised has occasioned anxious perplexity to many a student, learned and simple. For the first impression on the mind may very naturally be that the one Apostolic writer is, if not directly contradicting the other, yet seeking to counteract some popular distortion of the other's teaching. But the true answer to the riddle appears to lie in a very different quarter.

It has been shewn by Bishop Lightfoot * that the Faith of Abraham was a favourite topic for discussion among the Jewish Rabbis. Like St. Paul, but in a spirit widely different from his, they debated the precise connexion between Abraham's Faith and his acceptance before God. And their tendency was, in brief, to attach Abraham's salvation to his orthodox confession of the glory of JEHOVAH as the one true God; in fact, to his monotheistic creed. Thus the idea of Faith, to them, was precisely Creed. And their inference was that the supreme qualification for divine acceptance was truth of Creed, a thought which some of them pushed to the extent of at least suggesting that truth of Creed could atone for laxity of life.

Take these facts, and apply them to

* *Galatians*, Detached Note to Chapter iii.

St. James' words. Do they not at once illuminate his meaning? He illustrates (verse 19) his thought by an example: "Thou *believest,*" it is thy Faith, "that there is ONE GOD," or, better, "that GOD is ONE." This was precisely the supreme point of Jewish orthodoxy. The great words "Hear, O Israel, the LORD our God is one LORD,"* are words which to this day the devout Israelite desires to utter in the act of death, almost as a password to eternal peace. They are called the *Sh'ma,* which is the Hebrew for their first word, "*Hear,*" and the *Sh'ma* is the pious Jew's desired last utterance on this side death. Just this brief creed St. James quotes, and then says that "the devils themselves" are sound and orthodox upon it. But does it save them? "They believe —and tremble."

* Deuteronomy vi. 4.

Then, taking the word Faith in the sense thus put upon it by the Scribes —not by St. Paul,* but by the Scribes— he holds up to the light the tremendous fallacy of their teaching. He takes Abraham, and he takes Rahab, names both of which, in their widely different ways, were favourite examples with the Rabbis, and he shows how little their salvation was to be explained by a *Sh'ma,* however sublimely true.

They were saved by something, whatever it was, which moved their wills into the line of the will of God. Theirs was *an attitude* which led the one to lay his son upon the altar, and led the other to recognize in Israel the chosen people and to cast in her lot with them. In that sense truly they were "justified" in respect of something far

* Very probably St. Paul had not yet, by some years written his Epistle to the Romans.

other than only Creed, something which infallibly came out in action.

St. James was thus enforcing a truth quite as dear to St. Paul (when he too came to write about it) as to himself. It was the truth that theoretical orthodoxy, apart from effects upon the will, is futile. Not in the least degree would he be questioning the teaching that the sinful soul is put into a position of acceptance with God solely by vital connexion with His Son. Not in the least would he deny that this connexion is effected, absolutely and alone, not by personal merit, but by the Faith which means a trustful acceptance of the Son of God as our sacrifice. But his thought in this passage lay in a direction altogether different. He had in view the theory that Faith means not trustful acceptance, but orthodox adherence, and he warns his Hebrew readers that

Faith in that sense is not salvation. It may be held with perfect mental conviction, and yet the man may be lost.

Thus far we have considered in a merely critical way the use of Faith to denote Creed. In the New Testament we have called attention to its comparative rarity in that sense. And in the well-known paragraph of St. James we have seen (if the interpretation advocated is right) that this exceptional sense is used by the Apostolic writer rather as the sense adopted by the Scribes than as his own. He is arguing against them on their own ground, and so he uses their own terms in their own way. In one other passage at least (verse 15) he uses Faith in its more proper sense, that of reliance: "The prayer of *Faith* shall save the sick"—words which can only refer to the trustful attitude of those who take God at His word and plead His promises for an answer.

Some other passages in the Acts and Epistles call for other shades of explanation. Thus in Acts xvii. 31 we have *pistis* in the sense of a warrant or guarantee: "God hath given *assurance*" of the coming judgment "in that He raised Christ from the dead." Here the thought of reliance glides over into the thought of something given to secure reliance: a token, a pledge, a seal, making the promise more tangible for reliance to embrace. Again, in Rom. iii. 3 we have *pistis* in the sense of "good Faith," trustworthiness: "Shall their unbelief make *the Faith* of God of none effect?" Here once more we have a transition of thought from a primary to a secondary meaning, from trust to trustworthiness.

This last phrase, "the Faith of God,"

gives occasion for a remark on a class of passages where the same grammatical structure is used but where the primary sense of Faith is in place. Three such occur in the one chapter, Gal. ii. There, in verse 16, we read how man is "not justified by the works of the law, but by the Faith of Jesus Christ."; and, again, one line below, "that we might be justified by the Faith of Christ." In verse 20, one of the most pregnant sentences in St. Paul's writings, we read literally, that "I live by the Faith of the Son of God."

At first sight we may interpret such words to mean that it is by the "good Faith" of the Redeemer, by His trustworthiness, that we get our justification and our life. And most assuredly, from the supreme point of view, this is deeply true. But when we put these passages in line with St. Paul's general teaching about our salvation and its connexion with Faith I think we are reasonably sure that, if only the practice of Greek grammar will allow us to do so, we ought to explain the phrases to mean the trust which *takes hold of* the Lord, for peace and life.

And most certain it is that Greek grammar does allow of such an explanation of this genitive construction, this phrase, "the Faith of Christ." See, for example, Mark xi. 22. There the Greek runs, "Have Faith of God." Our English Bible rightly translates it and explains it by, "Have Faith in God." It is only an instance of the use of the genitive case in one of its most original and, so to speak, native meanings, the meaning of contact, adherence, grasp. "Faith of God" is trust in God, touching, clasping, grasping, uniting itself with, its glorious Object.

This, however, is only a note by the way.

One passage in St. Paul where Faith is named calls for special notice, for in some respects it seems to stand by itself. It is 1 Cor. xii. 9: "To another is given Faith, by the same Spirit." The Apostle here is reckoning up the mighty "gifts" of grace, the *charismata* as the Greeks call them, given by the exalted Lord through His Spirit to His Church. Among them are powers of utterance, powers of healing, powers of miracle, of prophecy, of the mysterious "tongues" and their interpretation. With these here he groups Faith. And of Faith he speaks, as he speaks of the other gifts, as a power granted not to all Christians but to some.

Just as not all but some had the "second sight" of the prophet, or the marvel-working touch of the healer, or the enraptured diction of the speaker with tongues, so not all—though all in question were true Christians—had Faith. It was a special "gift," and given to chosen receivers only. What can he mean? Without hesitation I reply that he is here taking Faith under an abnormal aspect. It is not possible that he means Faith in the sense of reliance upon the word of salvation, for that is the primary and vital requisite, the common "grace," of all true believers. Their very name, "believers," takes that for granted. The Apostle must mean here a special grant to the chosen Christian, a special faculty or exercise of reliance upon his Lord, such that his Faith shall show its power in ways distinctive and abnormal, bordering on the region of miracle and sign.

A modern instance has often occurred to me in illustration. It is that of the late Mr. George Müller, of Bristol. Through a long course of years he built up and maintained a great and beneficent work, his Orphanage, and from first to last his principle, strictly and most nobly followed out, was to use Faith in the living love, providence, and power of God as the agency for furnishing the money which was needed, and needed in very large sums, for the work. Müller was a bearer of the special gift of special Faith.

But I have said enough of the exceptional uses of the word Faith in the Apostolic writings. It remains only to call attention, in the light of these exceptions, to the rule. I do not hesitate to say that if I quoted in illustration of that rule I should have to transcribe an appreciable part of the whole body of the Epistles. Let me rather commend to the reader the attentive study of the prevalent use in them of Faith and of its exercise; I think he will find for himself that while the word Trust may be used in this vast majority of instances as the synonym of Faith, there is no other word which will do so. With the Apostles, not St. Paul only but St. Peter and St. John, Faith normally means Trust.

One great passage, and one only, will I note here for special attention. It is the opening words of that glorious eulogy of the Faithful, the eleventh chapter of the Hebrews. No word have I to say here of the insoluble problem of the authorship of that book of Scripture. Enough here to be assured, on the ground of its acceptance by the Church as Scripture, set beside its power to work divinely in human souls as only an Oracle can do, now through eighteen centuries of time, that it was by a Christian Prophet, if not by an Apostle, that the Lord gave it to the Church. But it is solely upon the words of the first verse of this eleventh chapter that I now pause, and on the description there given of what Faith can do.

"What Faith can do"; that is precisely what this verse tells us. "Now Faith is the substance * of things hoped for, the evidence of things not seen." This sentence has been sometimes taken to define Faith, as if it gave a precise account of what Faith is, in terms applicable to nothing else. If so, it would explain Faith to be something of a "second sight" in the sense which, in our opening chapter, we saw reason to reject.

But on reflection, surely, we shall find

* The Greek word, *hypostasis*, may perhaps be rendered "guarantee." We now know from recent investigations of the type of Greek used in the New Testament that such was a frequent meaning of the word in common life.

that it is not so. The phrase is akin rather to such a saying as that which tells us that "knowledge is power," where knowledge is not defined in its nature but described in its issues. So Faith, the trust of man in God, is described here in its mysterious potency. Let man have God's promise, and let man fully trust the Promiser, and then his Faith puts him in living contact with the distant hope, with the unseen glory; the believer clasping the Promiser is as if the hope was in his hands, the invisible bliss before his eyes.

So it was with Noah, Abraham, Moses, and all that goodly company. They knew their Lord, they took Him at His word—and the mighty promises were made present to them, through Faith. Yet was that Faith in itself no more, and no less, than the repose of trust on the word of the Trustworthy One.

FAITH . .
AND CREEDS

CHAPTER IV

FAITH AND CREEDS

"FAITH" and "THE FAITH." We have already considered the fact that here and there in the New Testament, not often but certainly here and there, *pistis* denotes what we may broadly call Creed rather than that reliance which is the native and natural meaning of the word. There is no need here to follow this out further as a question of language. But it suggests to us the close relation which lies between the two thoughts, the two things, Faith and the Faith, Faith and Creeds.

When we speak the word "Creed," taking it in its Christian sense, we recall at once the great historical Creeds of the Church, familiarly known to us as the Apostles' Creed, and the Nicene, and the Athanasian; all named in the eighth Article of the Church of England, all used in public worship according to the English Prayer Book.

It would be quite out of place here to treat these Creeds in detail as to their growth and history, extremely interesting as that history is. Most untimely it would be to enter on the thorny question of the suitability of the third great Creed, the "Athanasian," for recitation in public worship, and to discuss the meaning and bearing of the tremendous words of the verse which stands second in its psalm-like structure. Enough perhaps to say of it here that investigation seems to shew that the document took its origin in a period of severe persecution, when orthodox believers were fiercely assailed not by pagan but by heretical enemies; a thought which may explain the stern and ruthless warnings of the second verse and of others, whether or not it proves that the same tone is befitting under widely altered conditions of the Church.

Little need be said about the mere story of the great historical Creeds. We may remember in passing the curious fact that each one of the three bears a traditional name which is not strictly true to its probable history, though this fact need not in the least disturb us, with the Bible open, as to the sacred value of these "forms of sound words" which have for ages upon ages embodied the foundation truths of our belief. The "Apostles' Creed," as we have it, did not take its full present form till generations after the last Apostle fell asleep. The "Nicene Creed," as we recite it, was not shaped at Nicæa, in 325, but is probably the resultant of a blending of the Creed of Nicæa with other forms of Church confession. The "Athanasian Creed" was not the work of Athanasius, nor of his age; it arose at a later time and in another region than his.

Further, not one of the Creeds appears to have been intended at first for recitation in common worship. The "Apostles' Creed" was at first used at baptism alone. The "Nicene Creed" was framed, somewhat as our Articles and similar documents are framed, as a test of the orthodoxy of individuals—for example, of persons elected to the episcopate. The "Athanasian Creed," as we have seen, was very probably written and issued as a rhythmical watchword for the persecuted.

But these points are not vital to our immediate thought. We will take the Creeds here as we find them and as we use them, as they have been used so long within the great Christian community. We will go on to note some outstanding features common to them all and to weigh something of the significance of these. We will then reflect on the relation of such Creeds to Faith and of Faith to them.

First then we find that the Creeds are all primarily concerned with God, the supreme Object of trust and of adherence. We are taken by all of them straight to "the shadow of the Almighty," that shadow full of a light ineffable beyond. They "set Him before us" as the ultimate and sovereign Fact, of which we are sure, on which we rely. They lead us to regard Him, in one degree of detail or another, as He shines on us through a veil of mystery in the glory of His threefold Being—the Father Almighty, the Son eternal and incarnate, the divine Spirit of life and holiness.

Then, in all the Creeds alike, we find a space altogether special assigned to that sacred wonder, the Incarnation of the Son, His "becoming Man," while yet remaining for ever God; His taking our nature into eternal oneness with the supreme Nature; so that He, the One Person, the one Christ, is equally God the Son of God and Man the Son of Woman. In a profound connexion with the Incarnation the Creeds go on at once to the sacrificial Sufferings and Death of the incarnate Lord.

Significantly enough, in their statement of the foundations for our trust, they all pass direct from the Birth to the Death; they say not one word of what from other sides is so inestimably precious to the Christian, "the blessed steps of His most holy life," the story of Nazareth, Cana, Capernaum, and Bethany. For the basal rock of trust, "for us men and our salvation," is "the sacrifice of the death" of the Lord Jesus and "the glories that did follow."

His blessed life has another place, and another work. Its inexhaustible wonders of grace and power, unfolding the character of our Redeemer, putting us in contact with the spiritual power of His example, conveying to us His teaching, making us intimate with His will—all this forms the lifelong study and inspiration of the man who has laid hold on Christ for the forgiveness of sins and for conscious personal relations of peace with the Father in the Son.

But the Lord Himself in His incarnate glory, the Lord Himself in His sacrificial suffering, the Christ of Bethlehem and of Calvary—here lies the cause, the secret, the way, of that peace and life;

we need no elaborate proof of this when once we have spiritually seen ourselves. So the Creeds take us straight to the Cross, and then, through that "grave and gate of death" which the Crucified traversed for us, to the triumph of Resurrection, to the completion of Resurrection in Ascension, to the exaltation of the Risen One to the Throne, to His Coming to His Church again.

No part of the Apostles' and Nicene Creeds compares in detail with this "paragraph of redemption." It is the glowing centre of the whole matter of our belief. In its light we confess the glory of the Father not with a *mere* sense of mystery or of awe, but with the love of worshipping children, in and through our divine and human Brother, Sacrifice, and Head. In its light we go on to confess the glory and Godhead of "the Lord, the Life-giver," the eternal Spirit, not as an abstract wonder, but as the glory of Him through whom the Prophets spoke of the coming Christ and the Apostles spoke of the Christ now come, and who, dealing with our hearts and wills, gives us that life eternal which is theirs who "know the only true God and Jesus Christ whom He hath sent."*

Then, from God, the Three and One, creating, redeeming, life-giving, the Creed passes to Man. It speaks of the holy Catholic Church, the redeemed and believing community of Christian men, united in their countless individualities by the Spirit in the Son of the Father. It speaks of the Baptism which is the appointed door of open entrance into its membership, the God-given seal of the covenant of pardon, righteousness, and life, made with every true member in the

* John xvii. 3.

Triune Name. Lastly, it bids us be sure of that immortal future to which all that we can know, believe, and practise here is but the school and prelude —"the resurrection of the dead and the life of the world to come."

Thus the Creed calls us solemnly forth first to stand, or rather kneel, upon our foundation, upon our God, the Lord of creation, redemption, and life. Then upon that foundation it sets at once the walls which surround and protect Faith, the house and home of the Christian community, the Church. Lastly, above those walls it spreads the sky of hope, "that blessed hope," "the inheritance which fadeth not away."

One further word on the structure and phraseology of the two oldest Creeds. They are cast on the one hand into a form personal and individual; "I believe." They are used on the other hand in public worship, they are voiced by a congregation. Two sides of the Christian life are intimated thus. First, it is a life in which nothing—no, not the Church of God itself—must come between the individual and his Lord in the inmost relations of reliance. Secondly, the individual's contact with his God will never normally do its perfect work if it does not issue in fellowship with the community and contribute to the common life. And the common life on its part will contribute powerfully and with ever-growing benefit to the individual's contact with God in faith, hope, and love.

Action, reaction, interaction, will do a work whose issues cannot be calculated, as the man confesses his Faith in living reality "in the midst of the congregation," and the congregation in living reality, spiritual worship, makes its Faith felt around the individual.

What earnest believer has not known such experiences? Perhaps we have been "weary and faint in our minds," in a silent, solitary hour. We have risen on the morning of the Lord's Day burthened with the sense of sorrow, or of fear, or of sickening spiritual misgivings. We have betaken ourselves to Church, carrying the burthen still. And then—perhaps it is in some glorious minster, perhaps in the village church among the quiet fields, perhaps in the less beautiful sanctuary of "the unlovely street"—we have stood up with the congregation to recite the Faith, Apostolic or Nicene.

A strange magnetic encouragement has thrilled our spirits. The patent, objective fact of the public, unfaltering, utterance around us of the immemorial Creed has waked us up to realize in a quickened individual experience at once the massive greatness, and the daylight soberness, and the transcendent glory, of the Tenets which had seemed to fade and waver in our sad hearts. We have recited them one by one with a new certainty and life. And perhaps the quiet firmness of our own overheard utterance, mingling in the great unison, has carried the same sacred magnetism out to other hearts around us.

The Creeds, and all creed-like voices of the Church besides, the Doxology, the Te Deum, the Gloria in Excelsis, not to speak of the great modern hymns of Faith, the song of the Rock of Ages, or of the Wondrous Cross, or of the God of Abraham, have done and are doing work beyond all reckoning and all measure for individual Faith. They quicken its exercise by defining and accentuating its basis. They animate the man's confidence in Him whom they set forth by blending it with the confidence of the

Church, and of the ages. Even in the Christian's solitary hour they carry to him the reassuring voices of "his brethren who are in the world,"* till he says to his own soul, with a new decision of Faith, "I believe in God, the Father, Son, and Spirit; I believe in the resurrection of the dead and the life of the world to come."

* 1 Peter v. 9.

FAITH . .
AND PRACTICE

CHAPTER V

FAITH AND PRACTICE

FAITH, by the nature and necessity of the case, is practical. If true to its description, Faith is personal reliance on a Person, exercised by a living soul in a real life. It is an attitude taken and maintained with a view to the conditions of duty, labour, suffering, opportunity, faculty, which make the path of that real life what it is. It presupposes something of the unknown, the uncertain, the difficult, the perilous, as lying along that path. And the believer, the man of Faith, addresses himself to that path with the persuasion that the one true secret by which to tread it aright, and to attain at last its radiant end, is to keep in contact with the divine Guide, and to trust Him for leading and for power.

It is a frequent temptation in the Christian life to lose sight of this intended practical application of the gifts of grace. As a fact, the very purpose of God's endowment of us with His present peace and strength, in whatever form, is for use, for the needs of the present spot and the present day, such as they are to ourselves. Yet nothing is more common in even the earnest disciple's life than a failure, more or less, to realize this.

Sometimes the mind is dissipated and weakened by spending itself on dreams of imagined circumstance. Perhaps the fancy dwells on ambitious possibilities. We think what we could be or could do as Christians in some hour of glorious danger, in days of persecution, in view of a martyr's death, or again in face of a call to some great achievement for

God in life and labour, say in the missionary front of the campaign of the Church. Or perhaps, and probably much oftener with many of us, the line of thought is just the opposite. We conjure up conditions of difficulty, more or less possible, and meet them with our own weakness, and anticipate a failure and a fall. We waste feeling and thought upon useless contrasts and comparisons between ourselves and other Christian people, and between our lot and theirs. We imagine them succeeding amidst our circumstances, because of their better equipment, or ourselves doing much better amidst theirs, in which we think we see helps and facilities which are denied to us.

All this is sheer misuse of heart and mind. It must be put decisively away by the firm remembrance that our own conditions, as they surround us here and now, are the very field on which the grace of God, the God of grace in us, is to put forth virtue and to overcome. Let us come down from these idle flights in the clouds and feel the ground again. The task of to-day for me, the very next incident of work, of intercourse, of suffering or enjoyment, of love or loss, just as it arises for me, is the one possible, the one sacred, opportunity for my recollecting and using the gifts of God to me.

Be the limitations around me, and the acute sense of inadequacy in me, what they may, it is for me here, for me now, that my Lord in His grace and love exists. They may seem to be precisely the things which must isolate me from Him, so secular seems the position and so secular also the heart. But let those very facts be put beside the fact that I am His and He is mine, that I exist for Him and that He is pleased to give

Himself to me, and they become the occasions and opportunities of grace. They are hallowed into becoming the very scene of blessing.

"O that I had wings like a dove," to fly away from just these problems, above all to escape from my character, from myself! But just here is the moment for Faith. Let Faith call in God to meet my problems and myself. The sequel will be one of pregnant good, for it will run along the line of the will of God.

An illustration of the first magnitude, but applicable to our minutest trials as well as to our heaviest, is given us by St. Paul in 2 Cor. xii. 7–10 He opens to us there a short but wonderful chapter of his spiritual biography. In the midst of his largest labours, and just after a crisis of rapturous revelation, he was suddenly troubled with an intolerable access of bewildering and humiliating pain.

What it was precisely we shall never know, till we are permitted perhaps to ask him about it, face to face, under the trees of the Garden of God. But it seems certain that the evil was at once physical and spiritual, a withering malady in the body and, along with it and delivered through it, a direct assault on his spirit by wicked spiritual powers. Conditions of the very sort to wreck his missionary ministry burst suddenly upon him. He would infinitely rather they were otherwise. He would be miserable, he would be useless, if he remained as he was!

In this dark hour and with these dark thoughts he turned to his Lord, telling Him all, asking Him in an agony of petition for—other conditions. "I besought the Lord thrice that it might depart from me." We know the answer. The conditions, for the moment certainly, were left upon him, with all their weight of stress and suffering unchanged. But the suppliant was assured that Christ in him would more than meet them, and that this should be the secret of a spiritual growth and greatness in his experience which mere relief could not possibly bring. "My grace is sufficient for thee, for it is in weakness that my strength comes to its perfection."

We know the sequel. The Apostle did not merely endure, great as that issue would have been. It is a very great thing to "learn to suffer without crying."* But it is a greater thing by far to learn to suffer with an exulting consciousness of gain and growth. "Most gladly therefore will I rather glory in my weaknesses, that the power of Christ may rest upon me. Therefore I take

* *Lerne zu leiden ohne Klagen:* the motto of the late Emperor Frederick of Germany.

pleasure in weaknesses, for when I am weak then am I strong." So the Apostle emerged from the struggle "more than conqueror." Not only did the enemy prove powerless; a whole spiritual realm was annexed to the spiritual life of the distressed disciple.

True, the sufferer in this case was personally great, and the work was great, and the very evils had an aspect of sombre greatness in them. But the essence of the matter is independent of its scale. Here was a human heart crushed under difficulty, and here was the difficulty left as it stood, only transfigured into educative opportunity and spiritual triumph. And how? By the power of a trusted Christ—that is to say, by Faith. The man put Faith into practice under those well-nigh impossible conditions. And the incident formed a mighty spiritual epoch in the life; we need not be told how great the access would be from that hour, in the inner history of St. Paul, even to the end, in *the habit* of victory through Faith.

It is just this development of *the habit of believing* which we are to look for in the practice of Faith. In the spiritual life, as in the natural, there is a valid law of habit. We must not allow any other side of truth to obscure that principle. The strong certainty that our spiritual life is a divine gift, and that the Giver is able to do what He wills with it, and, if He so wills, to grant sudden growths in it out of His royal bounty, must not let us forget the law of spiritual habit.

As a fact, these epochs and critical moments in the spiritual life just referred to will nearly always, I venture to say, be found to stand related to something habitual which went before them as preparation. St. Paul's habit of prayer, for example, his formed instinct to turn to Christ under crushing need instead of letting the need merely paralyse him, led up in an organic order to the divine answer which suddenly glorified his misery into victory. Anywise, our immediate business in the spiritual life is to bring our spirit to meet the Divine Spirit, however true it is that He all the while "divideth to every man as He will." Therefore let us address ourselves to form the habit of Faith amidst "all the changing scenes of life," under the conditions of the common day as they come not to others but to us.

How shall we do so best? Upon the whole, in very simple ways. First of all, let us form the spiritual habit of "setting the Lord always before us." We can never too often remember, nor too simply, that the true power of true Faith lies in its Object. Therefore let us recollect the Object. Let us habitually say within the soul the creed of life: "I believe in God, in God in Christ, in the Christ of God."

"He lives, He loves, He knows;
Nothing that thought can dim;
He gives the very best to those
Who leave the choice to Him."

It is possible so to think that truth, and so to confess it, if only to ourselves, that it shall grow out of an act into a habit, and become the attitude and not merely a motion of the soul. We may contribute to the process in many ways. We may foster it by fresh thought, with prayer, upon the vast ranges of reason that gather round the certainty; by recalling and treasuring up the innumerable testimonies to the Fact of God borne to us by the experiences of the saints; by definite acts of devotion; by persistent companionship with the Bible; by use in spirit and in truth of the Sacrament of the Body and the Blood of the Son of God. But we are just now concerned most with simple acts of recollection of God and their development into a habit.

Many of my readers must know that memorable narrative, "The Practice of the Presence of God," the record of the experience of one Lawrence, the "lay-brother" of a French monastery in the seventeenth century, who developed to a noble degree and to great results of holiness the habit of recollection that "the Lord is near." Always, everywhere, as much in work-time as in the hour of prayer, as truly in the kitchen as in the chapel, he "remembered God" as present. His experience is for us also, if we also will seek it in humility and with practical resolution.

Let that habit be formed, and we shall already be far on the way to a developed habit of Faith exercised under the real needs of life. To recollect the neighbourhood of God, of our God, of the Father in the Son, the Son in the Father, brought to be not only near us but in our hearts by His Spirit—this is already to stand *habitually* ready to trust Him, and to speak to Him as those who trust. And this habituation of the soul to speak to Him, anywhere, at any moment, about anything, will be the natural process towards the habit of Faith in its mature and beautiful fulness.

It was well said by Charles Vaughan and also by Edward Clifford, both of blessed memory, that the inner surface of every true Christian life consists of "conversation with God." Our part is to maintain our side of the conversation, while we humbly listen for His. And His side not seldom will come to us in what, except to Faith, may seem a silence, but which to Faith will be a Presence, silent indeed, yet living, listening, and most loving, the supreme assurance of a divine watchfulness over us and a divine provision for us.

Come then, and let us converse with God, till the habit to tell Him everything and to trust Him in everything becomes inveterate. Let us take the very next opportunity to begin; the difficult work, the troublesome letter, the apparent conflict of duties, the narrowness of means, the death of the beloved, the isolation, the growing old and tired. A hundred difficulties are around us; but Faith, that is to say, God trusted, is a master-key for the prison-doors of life. *Solvitur ambulando,* it was said of old—the problem is solved by walking. We will extend the saying by two words: *Solvitur ambulando cum Deo*—the problem is solved by the walk of Faith with God.

FAITH . . .
AND CHARACTER

CHAPTER VI

FAITH AND CHARACTER

From a certain point of view and with watchful limitations we may affirm that the aim and function of true religion is the making of character.

The words do need limitation; they need all around them the recollection of yet greater truths. At the present day there is a strong and complex movement in thought and speech about religion which trends away from the eternal and the divine towards ideas too much bounded by "this present world" and by humanity as its inhabitant. One would think sometimes, as one reads or hears discourse upon religion, in undoubtedly Christian quarters, that religion exists ultimately to make this world a scene of universal enlightenment and comfort, and that when that end shall be attained religion will have won its victory and received its kingdom.

So far has such a tendency gone that it has come to be almost out of fashion, in many Christian pulpits, belonging to many Christian communions, to make much reference to a revealed eternal future. This is supposed apparently to be unpractical. Our concern is to be not with an invisible and, in many respects, unimaginable world to come but with the world visible and present. Not the gate of pearl, the street of crystalline gold, the river of life, and the trees which beside it bear their immortal fruits amidst their healing leaves, but the street, the lane, the slum of the modern town—this is the proper theme of the preacher. The miseries and wrongs around us, the responsibility of the prosperous community for their existence, the duty to work for their cure, here lies the true line of speech.

It is the case, too, if I mistake not, that in large areas of Christian thought and teaching a most inadequate place is given to the supreme and sovereign glory of God. Very little is said now in the sense of that memorable answer to the question, "What is the chief and highest end of man?"—"*To glorify God, and to enjoy Him for ever.*" In a way strange and disquieting, when we come to think of it, if we retain any reverential confidence in Scripture as revelation, it would seem to be assumed that rather God exists for man than man for God; that the highest aim of man is to realize himself, and that the work, I had almost dared to say the duty, of God is to enable man to do so.

In all these types of thought there lie embedded large fragments and elements of truth. It is indeed imperative upon Christian men to care very greatly indeed about misery and wrong around them. No words of mine are strong enough to emphasize as I would that claim upon the conscience of the Church and of the disciple. And it is indeed the sacred duty of man, made in God's image, to seek to realize in humbleness, fear, and hope, his own glorious ideal. But these all-important duties can never be done rightly while the spiritual solar system is wrongly interpreted, and man is practically made its sun and God its planet; nor while the being born for immortality is allowed to think that his ideal can ever be approached while he declines to look at, and ultimately and steadfastly to live for, the things not seen which are eternal. And assuredly it will be found that precisely in proportion as God resumes His right supremacy in thought and worship, and heaven its right place in living hope, the life that now is, and the humanity that is passing through it, will best "come to their own" in *present* conditions of righteousness, purity, and love.

But this being said, and it seemed worth the while to say it, I return to the assertion of the unspeakable importance of the making of character, and the greatness of it as an aim of religion. Let us with worshipping watchfulness set the Lord God upon the throne in all our thoughts. Let us be perfectly sure that man's highest glory is to exist altogether for Him. But then, and therefore, let us remember the mysterious greatness and significance of man, who was created in the image of God on purpose that he might exist worthily for Him. Let us see in that very fact the motive which is to animate man with the ambition to develope character to its ideal, not that he may "possess himself," but that he may be the fitter to be the possession of his God.

Such a purpose is put before us in Apostolic terms in a memorable passage in that most moving of dying letters, the Second Epistle to Timothy. There, in the second chapter (verses 20, 21), St. Paul lays it upon Timothy, and through him upon every Christian, to make it his ambition to be "a vessel unto honour, sanctified, meet for the Master's use, prepared unto every good work." The man is to find his true ideal in being the property, the implement, of Another, of his divine and autocratic Possessor, his *Despotês*, if I may transcribe the significant Greek word. But how is this to be? From the man's own point of view, it is to be by the freest possible resolve to purify and elevate his own character. "If a man purify himself from these things," if he cleanse his spirit of wrong motives, his life of evil habits, then "he shall be a vessel unto honour." Is not this just to say in other words that he is to seek by every means the fulness of the Christian character, on purpose that he may be a better and more usable implement of the will of Christ?

Now to such a growth and fulness of our true selves a potent means is Faith. Again we remember what Faith is. It is personal trust in a person, exercised by a living soul in a real life. Such trust, in its successive acts, will have its particular and immediate aims and effect. But as the acts collect themselves into a habit they will have results far transcending any immediate occasion. They will be a power in and on the character.

As one result, they will deepen and

develope *the consciousness of dependence.* Cultivating the habit of trust in a known, worshipped, beloved Master, the disciple will more and more consciously find and feel his centre of repose and strength not in himself but in "Him in whom he has believed."

Faith, the act and the habit, will have thus a profound influence on that side of Christian character which is at least as vital as any other, its side of humility. As necessary as the root to the plant, as necessary as the foundation to the structure, so is humility to the organism of the Christian character. It is humility at the basis of all other characteristics which gives its peculiar quality, its *Eigenart,* as the Germans would call it, to strictly *Christian* virtue ; to the courage, for example, to the endurance, to the purity of principle, to the hatred of evil in every form, which is shewn by the true disciple. And the true secret for the presence and growth of true humility resides just here, in the felt and cherished fact of an entire dependence upon Another, and that other—Jesus Christ. It is no product of an artificial and studied self-abasement, an elaborate practice of certain definite humiliations. Such things, especially when they take shape in acts and practices which in the least degree tend to make *a display* of "voluntary humility" (Col. ii. 18), can very easily slide into a subtle but dangerous form of self-exaltation, hard, cold, ambitious, untrue, tainted with a pharisaic readiness to compare self favourably, however secretly, with others.

But the humility "which is from above" is a very different thing. It rises out of a close contact between the disciple and the Master, the vassal and his Lord. That contact keeps the man always *and naturally* low and little in his own esteem, yet in a manner which has not the slightest connexion with debasement. It means the habitual consciousness of an immeasurable difference, an infinite superiority in the glorious other Person. But this consciousness is so vitally penetrated with a concurrent certainty of connexion, of affinity, that there is nothing in it of repulsion. Rather it involves an indescribable attraction, and the reception into the whole humbled being of the uplifting and ennobling "power of Christ."

This contact is maintained above all by the exercise of Faith, the personal trust of the dependent Christian in the personal Christ. As this trust is habitually put forth upon its Object, its effect upon the believing heart is always formative of the true humility which we have tried to describe. At the basis of the man's being he is always thus being "rooted downwards," not into weakness but into power. He is always being drawn away from self-complacency into contentment with his Lord, from the unsettling pains of mortification, the other side of vanity, into rest in the greatness and goodness of His will. He becomes in character one of the strong and happy people of whom the young shepherd of the fair Valley of Humiliation sings, in the Pilgrim's Progress:

> "He that is down needs fear no fall,
> He that is low no pride;
> He that is humble ever shall
> Have God to be his Guide."

Yes; because the dependent spirit is the meek spirit. And "the meek will He guide in judgment, the meek will He teach His way."

It is obvious that Faith will have a large range of working, besides that just now indicated, in the making of the Christian character, though all such other workings will be found to be related to this, the deepest. It is certain that the habit of Faith will tend directly to develope in the character that "*patience* which is almost power," which in fact is power, if it is patience in its Scriptural sense, that is to say, the persistency which rises up and goes on again. The heart's habitual reference of its problems, speculative, emotional, practical, not to the often noisy authority of its own cogitations but first and most to a present Friend who is at once perfectly wise, perfectly powerful, and all-kind, will promote a "quietness" as well as "confidence" which will preclude panic, and haste, and self-will, and will have a wonderful faculty for uphill paths and tiring roads.

A soldier, reliant on a perfectly and justly trusted leader, will need very little exhortation to remember the value of discipline and the duty of obedience even amidst alarming difficulties. His trust schools him of itself into orderliness and courage.

Have we ever studied in personal examples the character-making power of Christian Faith? We may very possibly have known by living intercourse some eminent examples of "the life, walk, and triumph of Faith"—eminent, perhaps, not in the least by a wide reputation but by a holy fulness of contact with God viewed best *behind* the more public scenes of life. Christian history is full of illustrations of the power which a trust in "Him who is invisible" has over the whole attitude of the personality towards all that is most visible—chastening, calming, elevating, detaching from the encumbrances of self-will, while yet the will is nerved and developed to its utmost for unselfish action or endurance by a repose upon the will supreme. But we need not go to public records only for such phenomena. I myself have seen them where the Muse of History never watches and transcribes—"in the huts where poor men lie," in the walks of unnoticed pastoral devotion, in the life of the self-forgetting mother, in the sick-chamber where the outward man indeed did perish but the inward man grew day by day into a new symmetry and strength. The secret was everywhere open, and everywhere the same. In its pure essence it was Faith. It lay in the formative power of a perpetual contact with the trusted Christ.

FAITH . . .
AND TRAINING

CHAPTER VII

FAITH AND TRAINING

THE work of Faith in the making of character has just engaged our attention. The matter now before us stands in the closest relation to this; indeed, it is an extension and continuation of it. But taken as I propose to take it, giving a special reference to the word Training, the theme has an import of its own and may stand by itself.

Training is a word which by its nature looks and reaches forward into the future. We are put under training always for something not present but to come; in order to be and to do what is "not seen as yet." The athlete with his preparatory exercises, the soldier getting ready for the campaign, the intending teacher still under teaching in class or college, are all full of a prospect; they are living, learning, bearing, practising, not for to-day but for to-morrow. And each and all of them, if they are worthy learners, and handled by a trainer of recognized capacity, are ready and willing to go through many things in their training whose utility is obviously not immediate. They know that somehow it bears upon the end, upon the goal. In the words of the Greek poet,* "they carry Faith with them, for the sake of the end."

Even so with Christian Faith, because it is Faith, and true to its nature. It has indeed an immediate issue in each moment of its exercise; it is put forth to be our victory in this temptation, our strength for that labour, our cheer and comfort under the particular pain or loss

* Sophocles, *Electra*, 535: τῷ τέλει πίστιν φέρων.

which encounters us to-day. But all the while it is doing its larger and more ultimate work by training us for another scene, for the conditions of to-morrow. As with the making of character in general, so it is with this special work of training. We are being equipped and developed by the exercise of personal trust in a personal Lord here for nothing less than the exercise hereafter of the powers of "an endless life."

I speak here particularly and almost only of that life. There is of course a constant need of moral training, all along our way, for the futurities of this life, if I may use the phrase. The thoughtful young scholar, in however limited a measure, knows something of this, and sets himself the better for it to the dry and thorny work of mastering the grammar of a language, dead or living. He is told by his trusted teacher—the teacher, if he wishes to ally his pupil's heart with his intellect, will be sure to tell him so—that this uphill road, with its toilsome steps and slippery and dark places, will reward his patience in the end. It will put him in possession and command of a great and spacious literature. It will also prove to have drilled his reason, and to have disciplined and refined his mental perceptions, in ways and degrees which, for all the intellectual duties of his after years, will prove valuable beyond his present dreams.

Such unlooked-for results, scarcely imaginable to the student at the time, do often follow from the training of just such studies as we have been thinking of. It was said a few years ago by an eminent medical teacher that among his most receptive students he often found men whose earlier education had run along the old classical lines. Training in the field of grammar, with a view to accuracy, thoroughness, keenness of observation, had brought the mind to a high proficiency and efficiency in the exercise of the same faculties in the field of medicine.

So the Christian man, perhaps the Christian young man or young woman, "acting Faith," to use the old phrase, upon some limited and humble matter, to-day and then again to-morrow, may very likely be in training, from the divine point of view, for precisely the same action ten years hence upon matters which shall affect the very greatest interests in the service of God and man. The scholar has learnt the holy art of trusting in the dark "in a few things," and then he is promoted, not by accident, but as one whom the Master has trained on purpose for it, to do the like "in many things." And the many things are done all the more safely, all the more fruitfully, because of the days of homely discipline which went before.

Take such possibilities with you in your thought to-day, young disciple, and the very thought will pass upward into Faith. You will trust, in front of the veil which hides your future; you will rely on the will and skill of your divine Teacher and Trainer to be preparing you through your trust in Him now for your larger trust in Him then. The whole of your life to-day will be a walk of Faith towards the victories of Faith to-morrow.

But let us pass now from "the futurities of this life" and think a little of the future on which they all converge, the future of the life eternal.

Here first let us place before ourselves, by a deliberate act of Faith, the certainty that that life is to be, and is to be for us. We need to do this often in our difficult day, when "intimations of immortality" are, for innumerable minds, grievously disturbed and, as it were, muffled by loud voices of current thought—or often rather by the failure of genuine thought amidst the hurry of life, perhaps even amidst the over-pressure of the machinery of education. Let us resolve to set the eternal prospect before us. To that end we welcome every lawful aid; the witness of our nature (a vital matter) to our relation as persons to the Infinite Person; the testimonies of mind, of conscience, of love, of

> "Thoughts whose very sweetness yieldeth proof
> That they were born for immortality."

But welcoming these helps, recognizing, among other things that if we had not a nature capable of "thoughts that wander through eternity" the voice of the Eternal Himself would find in us no spiritual ear to receive it, and so would be no sound to us at all, let us then all the more listen to Him, with the simplest possible Faith, when He tells us of the eternal life. Let us approach Him afresh in His incarnate Son. Let us look anew into "the face of Jesus Christ," shewn in the mirror of the Gospels, of the Epistles, of the whole Bible, and realize anew its all-sufficient self-evidence. Then let us weigh anew the words of those sacred lips: "He that believeth in me shall never die"; "Neither can they die any more"; "This is the life eternal, to know the only true God and Jesus Christ whom He hath sent."

Let us ponder the parables in which He turns the transcendent mystery of the unseen life into the current coin of concrete imagery; "the bosom" of Abraham, the Garden of God, the bridal feast, the heavenly garner, and, not least, that picture which shews us the invisible life on the one hand as a scene of diligent, fruitful, elevated service—"Have thou authority over ten cities"—and on the other hand as one ineffable consciousness of embracing and, as it were, whelming gladness—"Enter thou into the joy of thy Lord." Let us recollect so, and listen so, and come away with a fresh and inextinguishable certainty that Heaven is not dream but fact; a certainty received direct by Faith, for it lies involved in personal trust in the personal promise of the eternal Son.

Then, secondly, let us remember with distinctness and decision that that life bears an organic relation to this. Here again reason, in its largest and deepest sense, has much to say to us. But here again the highest act of reason is to pass upwards into Faith, and to take its certainty from the lips of Christ and His messengers. "Thou hast been faithful in a few things; I will make thee," in sequel, in consequence, after that educative exercise below, "ruler over many things"; "He that soweth to the Spirit shall of the Spirit reap life eternal". "Our light affliction which is but for a moment worketh out for us a far more exceeding and eternal weight of glory"; "Be followers of them who through Faith and patience inherit the promises."

The whole witness of the Lord and the Apostles, speaking to our deepest spiritual reason, assures us that "that world" is no isolated thing which merely happens to come after this, but that it grows out of this and is its flower. Put otherwise, the immortal is trained into receptivity for the bliss of immortality by the processes of heavenly grace in this the mortal prelude.

Is it not manifest how much of these processes takes effect, by the nature of the case, through Faith? "We walk," says the Apostle (2 Cor. v. 7), to render him literally, "by means of Faith, not by means of object seen." And surely he means to give us that fact not as a mere fact, but as a condition of our life below, full of significance and purpose. In words which occur in the near previous context of that sentence (2 Cor. iv. 17, 18) he makes that aspect of the thought still plainer. For we may paraphrase those verses somewhat thus, without outrunning the guidance of the delicate Greek: "Our trials here, relatively light and transient, are training us up to an endless experience of solid bliss, *keeping in view as we do* not the things seen but the things not seen"; or, in other words, walking as we do by Faith, not by sight.

The negative structure of the Greek there * is such as to convey precisely the thought that the *not* looking at the things seen, but the looking rather at the unseen, is a formative condition to the saint's finding at last that his present trials have been all the while ripening the harvest of his radiant life above. It is *as* he practises the vision of the unseen, taking his Lord at His mere word, and venturing upon it, step by step—steps that "fall on the seeming void and find the rock beneath"—that he is being educated, matured, into the being *capable of* "that world and the resurrection of the dead."

For that long life of bliss, which assuredly in its details "doth not yet appear," transcending not our experience only but our present faculties of comprehension, the man is being prepared pre-

* Μὴ σκοπούντων, not οὐ σκοπούντων.

cisely by his being required to take its glories for true, and for infinitely desirable, and worth all the trials and tears of the pilgrimage, without any evidence whatever from the senses, or the sensations. Only the antecedent discipline of the life of Faith, with its stern yet most gracious and loving treatment of the being, can lift it into an adult spirituality such that it can be trusted at last, and for ever, to "see face to face," to "know even as we are known," to look with such unveiled directness upon the supreme and eternal Beauty that the blessed "name" shall be legible "on the foreheads" of the glorified—CHRIST shining in His perfectness out of the undying personality of the Christian who is "for ever with the Lord."

Then at length, relatively to the experiences of time, Faith will have done its perfect work and give place to beatific sight. Not, surely, that Faith will have no place in the life of glory. The Apostle says nothing like that in 1 Cor. xiii. 11; rather he intimates a permanence for Faith and Hope as truly as for Love. But the place and function of it will be altered; it will be subordinate then as not before. For ever the Blessed will *trust* the eternal Love. But they will do so only with joy, never with effort, never with failure. For in the Holy City they will "walk by sight"; "they will see Him as He is." Their reliance will be a blessed and perpetual repose,

> "Where faith is sight, and doubt is o'er,
> And pain a nothing of the past,"

nothing, except for its results in a full capacity for the life in which at last man can be trusted, without its discipline, to be true for ever.

So let us set out afresh to "walk by Faith." Let us take our training with a "hope full of immortality." That hope, if we read the Apostle aright in the great words we have lately quoted, will begin to be realized in the moment of the believer's death. For the spiritual logic of 2 Cor. v. 6–8 delightfully compels us to such a conclusion. How does the deep and gracious argumentation run? It regards our present state, our sojourn in "the earthly house of this tabernacle," as conditioned by the two facts that in it we are "away from our home with the Lord" (*ἐκδημοῦμεν ἀπὸ τοῦ κυζίου*), and that we "walk by Faith not by object seen" (*οὐ διὰ εἴδους*). In contrast stands the coming life, when the spirit's "absence from home" shall be reversed; "quitting home in the body," we shall, evidently as the other side of the same experience, "get home to the Lord." We cannot be wrong in taking for granted the concurrent reversal of the other condition also of our life in the body. The pilgrim, passing hence, will wake up in that Home, in that Presence, to "walk by object seen," not after an interval of shadows but at once.

He shall "never see death" (John viii. 51). For just then and there, face to face, he "shall see the King in His beauty."

FAITH . . .

AND FORGIVENESS

CHAPTER VIII

FAITH AND FORGIVENESS

"I BELIEVE in the forgiveness of sins." This is a primeval article of the formulated Christian Creed. It could not be otherwise. For the fact that man needs forgiveness is a deliverance of man's inmost consciousness. However dimly illuminated that mysterious element of it, Conscience, may be, it bears persistent witness to the fact that man is not true to his ideal; that man is not right with the moral law which, more or less, he discerns above him and within him; that he is in some dark sense an offender who needs to be forgiven.

This voice from within man, greatly varying in detail under the vast variety of human conditions, including the long stages of the development of the race, yet always in some inmost elements the same, is amply responded to in Scripture. There indeed, in Old Testament and in New, "in sundry times and in divers manners," by precept, by story, by rite and ceremony, by tenderest appeal, by warning unutterably grave, by disclosures of the human heart, by visions of the glory of God, the thought of man's fault, demerit, wrong, guilt, is pressed on the reader.

And the progress and upward movement of the Biblical Revelation only serves to deepen this formidable conviction. There are aspects of things which in a certain sense that Revelation, having once dealt with them and made use of them, leaves behind; concessions to human rudeness and as it were infancy of soul, allowances for "times of ignorance" and for "hardness of hearts." But in this matter of conviction of sin, Revelation, the more it advances, speaks with a voice always more penetrating, more severe. That man is fallen from his moral ideal, that he is guilty before a perfectly holy law and Judge, that forgiveness, if it is to be had at all, is a vital necessity for man, comes out in the New Testament even more fully than in the Old. And nowhere in the New does it come out more largely and more awfully than in the personal teaching of our Lord Jesus Christ.

It is hardly necessary to say that we have need to recall this broad fact of Christianity to-day with a resolved and solemn vigilance. Almost as if by a general "unconscious cerebration," the very notion of moral wrong has come to be widely enfeebled among us, and a loose tolerance in respect of it is dangerously abroad. Above all the recognition of wrong *as guilt,* as a something which violates eternal statute-law and calls for retributory judgment if it does not find forgiveness, is out of fashion in the current thought even of the Christian Church. To a certain extent we are aware that wrong within us is a slavery, a pollution, a disquiet. But very much less are we alive to the fact, taking Christian circles as a whole, that this same wrong, if it is not to banish us from the peace and light of God in a very stringent sense indeed, must if possible be forgiven.

Such a change in moral "cerebration," let us be quite sure, is not an advance but a retrogression. It is not connected with upward movements of the mind and will towards loftier standards and nobler conduct. Rather it is the index of a slackening of idea and purpose about duty, virtue, temperance, righteousness, a lowered estimate of the supremacy of the moral over the material, the eternal over the temporal. This is a decline, a deterioration, of the subtlest and most fatal sort. It may coincide with extraordinary advances in the knowledge of matter and force, with an even bewildering influx upon us of inventions and improvements, with wireless telegraphs and perfectly dirigible airships, with a ceaseless abbreviation, so to speak, in these and similar examples, of space and time. But the toleration of sin, the acceptance of a neutral view of right and wrong, the contented oblivion of "temperance, righteousness, and judgment to come," must mean, all the while and none the less, a cancer at the vitals of human society and of the individual man. He may improve conditions around him, in the sense of a growing mastery and ease amidst them, and that to an indefinite degree, but he will be himself a decaying thing in the midst of the conditions, dying by a moral atrophy.

The greater, then, is the need that the Church, and the Christian, should recur continually to-day to the supreme revelation of sin and of righteousness given us by the Incarnate Lord. Nothing will take the place of that as an antidote to this deep evil of our time. From the Prophets who led up to Him, from the Apostles whom He sent out to unfold His glory and His truth, and from His sacred Self above all, we need continually to renew and deepen our dread of sin, our awe in face of judgment, and the conviction that forgiveness is our vital need.

As we study the Biblical doctrine of sin and pardon, we shall be sure to notice one important side of it. I mean, that in it the idea of God's forgiveness is such that it transcends what commonly forgiveness means and includes something nobler and greater still. This something is, in the language of theology, Justification. In words more familiar and of the common day, we may call it the Welcome, the Acceptance, of the guilty.

It differs from forgiveness, as we have said, by transcending it. It does not contradict it; it includes it, being a kindred but greater thing. Forgiveness remits penalty; it allows the offender to depart; at least it need imply no more than this. God's acceptance of sinful man does this—and very much more. It welcomes him to draw near, it beckons him in, it casts arms of love around him, it bids him be at home. In Christ's great parable the Prodigal was indeed forgiven the gross sin of his vicious and heartless prodigality. But that was not all. He might have been forgiven—and yet kept at a certain distance from his father, at least for a while. But not so; he was accepted. He was met with an embrace and led into a festival. He was bidden to be much more at home than ever.

Such is the Justification, the Acceptance, the Welcome, offered to sinful man by the very God who is of "purer eyes than to behold iniquity." There is a profound response and harmony between the tremendous energy of His condemnation of sin and this positive and infinitely gracious welcoming of the sinner. And the New Testament dwells on nothing with more fulness of teaching, and more light, and more love, than on the "way of peace" by which this gracious welcome travels and is poured out; that is to say, on the sacrificial sufferings of the Son of God, the atoning Death, the Propitiation for our sins, the

Redemption through the blood of the Lamb, the vicarious Passion of that Sufferer on whom "the Lord laid the iniquity of us all."

It is no part of my task here to attempt in any detail to set out the theology of the Atonement. And if it were my task, my very first care of all would be to emphasize to the utmost the inscrutable element of the wonderful truth. All analogies, all illustrations, sooner or later fail us, just because the Self-Sacrifice of the Son of God on our behalf, as we stand and gaze upon it in the glass of Scripture, is a thing unique and transcendent. But I must with humility avow that for me time only deepens the awed and rejoicing convictions of earlier years, reached not without great inward questionings, that, in the words of Harold Browne,* "the

* *Messiah Foretold and Expected,* ad finem.

word vicarious may not come fully up to what is revealed to us of the Passion, but that which is revealed of the Passion at least comes up to the word vicarious."

But now, what has Faith to do with this great thing, our "redemption in His blood, even the forgiveness of sins"?

It is most certain, as we listen to the Apostles and their Master, that Faith has to do with it, and in a way profound and vital. The sublime Redemption is set out before us, in all its majesty and its mercy, as "not according to our works"; it is the act, the gift, of God alone. But then we on our part are asked, commanded, to take action towards it. That action is—Faith. And the Faith in question is illustrated and exemplified, as if on purpose, by almost every incident in the Gospels where our Lord actually confers

His blessings.* His common, His normal requirement for a beneficial contact with Himself is just that personal trust in a Person which we have seen to be the native meaning of Faith.

That trust was exercised by the centurion who sought healing for his servant, by the Syrophenician mother, by the blind suppliants and by the paralysed, by the nobleman at Cana, by Martha at the tomb; and it, precisely this trust, was met by the gift of God. So with spiritual needs and maladies. "He that believeth on Him is not condemned," "shall never die," "is passed from death unto life." "We have access by Faith into this grace wherein we stand, and rejoice in hope of the glory of God." These illustrations can be multiplied indefinitely from the Gospels and the Epistles.

* See p. 34.

What is the account of this, so far as in reverence we can trace it out? The answer here must be brief; suggestive at the best; exhaustive it can never be.

And first, and most certainly, the account of it is *not* that Faith acts as a merit, as a deserving consideration, for the sake of which comes to us the "unspeakable gift." The trust of the drowning man in the life-belt, or in the life-boat, is no virtue and has no merit. It means a saving contact; that is all. With a grammatical precision which conveys inestimable spiritual truth the eleventh Article of the English Church takes care of this side of the matter. There the Latin runs that we are saved "*propter* meritum Christi, *per* fidem": "*on account of* the Lord's merit, *through* Faith in Him."

But now, what positive fitnesses can we see in Faith that it should mean "a saving contact" of the guilty soul with Christ in His sacrifice for us?

I reply, for one thing, that Faith, as we have just seen, is altogether not meritorious. Put this otherwise: trust brings nothing—in order that it may take all. It is an empty and therefore capacious hand. It is eyes which look wholly out upon Christ, and therefore wholly away from the sinner who looks out. It is the stepping of both feet, with all the weight they carry, upon the Rock of Ages. It is a contact as direct as possible, "nothing between."

Richard Hooker, in his massive *Discourse of Justification*, examines the contention of the Roman theologians that, while the medieval Church demanded many "works" as conditions of contact with the great Sacrifice, the Protestant conveniently, and to the large relief of spiritual indolence, reduced all such ways, works, merits, to one work—Faith. He gravely repudiates the charge, answering that in strictness we make Faith no virtue, nor merit, nor work, whatever. Work we preach indeed, but *in another place.* "Salvation by Faith" is but a shorter phrase for salvation by a trusted Christ. "God," he writes, "doth justify the believing man, yet not for the worthiness of his belief, but for the worthiness of Him which is believed."

Next, and therefore, we observe that the whole tendency of Scripture in this matter is to use just such phrases as to guide Faith straight to Christ our Sacrifice, not to our theories thereupon considered in themselves. It never bids us "believe in justification by Faith." It says, in countless varieties of expression, "Believe on the Lord Jesus Christ, and thou shalt be saved." It shows us the atoning Lamb, and bids us, not defend a theological position but lay the hand in confession and trust upon His sacred head.

Finally, and in close connexion with this last aspect of the matter, the work of Faith can be traced along what may be called the mystical path of the revealed salvation of man. Faith in the Son of God is, *ipso facto*, a spiritual contact with Him, living and life-bringing. In the luminous mysticism of the Scriptures a great place is taken by the truth of the Mystical Union. The Lord's parables of the vine and of the royal marriage, St. Paul's parables of the body and the limbs, and the head and the limbs, throw that truth into concrete forms. The phrase so often recurring (when the Greek is literally rendered), to "believe *into* Christ," to "believe *into* His Name," intimates the same truth every time. When we read, as we do in the Greek (Eph. iv. 32), that "God *in Christ* forgave you," we have it presented to us in precisely the connexion which is before us now; union with the Redeemer provides the spiritual *place* of forgiveness.

And what, from our side, is the bond which binds us into that union, so that Christ and His member, Christ and His Bride, are one? It is Faith. "Lord, I believe"; that is the word of espousal spoken to Him. And in that espousal the interests of the two sides merge and are at one. The burthen of the Christian is assumed by Christ; the wealth of Christ, carrying in it as an integral part "His meritorious death and passion," accrues to the Christian. It is mystery, but it is truth, truth of law and truth of love. Faith, our unifying contact with our Lord, because it possesses us of Him, makes us, in Him, sinners that we are, welcome in a more than pardon to the Father's home.

FAITH . . .
AND PURITY

CHAPTER IX

FAITH AND PURITY

BUT is the forgiveness and the welcome of the guilty the total of Redemption, Omega as well as Alpha for the soul? It is sometimes laid at the preacher's door that he says this, or implies it; that when he has explained, in the footsteps of St. Paul, that "God justifieth the ungodly," he has told us the whole message of the Gospel. This indeed is a charge not likely to be made often in our day, when the pulpit, as a rule, is very much more reticent than it was on the whole subject of guilt and its gracious remedy. But very frequently in a recent generation the accusation was heard. And sometimes there was reason in it; the teacher did sometimes treat forgiveness less as the threshold of the divine message than as its all in all.

Even to-day the expositor who sees and who expounds the need, the mystery, the glory, of the free welcomes of the Gospel, cannot, if he is jealous for the whole truth of his Master, too watchfully and too insistently explain that the divine purpose in the very act of forgiveness is to go on to transform the will, to purify, to sanctify, the man.

"Holiness, without which no man shall see the Lord"—such is the objective of the Gospel. Does man ask, as his final bliss, to "see God"? He must be "pure in heart." "There shall in no wise enter into" the city of the saints "anything that defileth." "Be not deceived; God is not mocked."

It is possible, for purposes of study, to isolate the wonderful phenomenon of a free forgiveness and of our acceptance for the "alone merits" of the crucified Lord, and to set it out by itself. I have attempted this just now in a simple way, in the study of Faith and Forgiveness. But what is possible for purposes of study is quite impossible in act and life, if that life is indeed Christian; that is to say, if it is lived along the line of the redeeming will of God. He who "gave Himself for us," bearing our sins, taking our liability, did it not only that we might be exempted from a capital sentence on the soul. He suffered that (Titus ii. 14) "He might redeem us from all iniquity, and purify us to Himself, a people of His own possession, zealous of good works."

The profound paradox of Biblical Christianity is that, instead of ending, *it begins* with its "abundant pardon." In the old familiar phrase of evangelistic preachers, it bids the man not work up to pardon but work up from it. The oblivion of that paradox is the subtle drawback upon the full efficacy of the labours and witness of many an earnest pastoral teacher. He needs to weigh again the terms of that "New Covenant" which the Lord, about to suffer, inaugurated (Luke xxii. 20) with the eucharistic chalice.

For what, when we come to study them, are those terms? First, "Their sins I will remember no more." Then, and only then, such is the divine order, "I will put My laws in their hearts," that is to say, I will transfigure their wills into unison with Mine. Such was the prophetic promise (Jer. xxxi. 31).* It took the Incarnation and the Cross to explain it;

* In the order *of mention* of the contents of the New Covenant, the transformed will comes first and the forgiveness last, but the order *of thought* is the other way: "I will put My laws in their hearts . . . *for* their sins I will remember no more."

but that explanation lies before us now. The glory of the New Covenant is open to us as we "survey the wondrous Cross" and present ourselves there to the power of the eternal Spirit.

Let us approach our present theme, the relation of Faith to purity, to holiness of heart and life, with these recollections about the true aim of the Gospel of redemption. That aim, let us be perfectly sure, never *terminates* in safety, immunity, or even gladness. The Gospel does indeed reveal for the faithful a safety, an immunity, free, large, and wonderful, and this is meant to be the secret, in part, of a "joy unspeakable." But the pardon of the Gospel is nothing but a first long step towards the production of a moral conformity to the will of God in the whole spiritual being of the forgiven, and its joys are inseparable from that conformity. Here, in the transfiguration of the will, we see the end indeed. Here thought rests satisfied, and conscience is fully met, and hope settles upon its centre. And the man, once really awake, cannot look lower than this. He must, by a moral necessity, amidst the largest and most rejoicing certainty of his unreserved acceptance for the sake of his Redeemer, and in union with Him, "hunger and thirst" for nothing less than this—to "purify himself even as He is pure."

"Good works," says the twelfth Anglican Article, "spring out necessarily of a true and lively Faith, insomuch that by them a lively Faith may be as evidently known as a tree discerned by the fruit." True words; yet (if this may be said with loyal reverence by a Churchman) the true words seem hardly adequate to the whole truth, to the whole profound relations of the matter. They leave us almost with the impression that "good works," or, in other words, a life lived true to God, fulfil their main function for the worker by satisfying him that his Faith has vitality, and so that he is safe. But the fact of the matter is that the worker exists for the "good works" as for his true end. They are not merely the gardener's label certifying the goodness and value of the tree. They are the fruit for which the tree was planted, for which it lives, without which it would be only a cumberer of the ground. We are saved—to serve.

And now, what is the relation of Faith to the production of purity of heart, purity of life, Christian holiness? That Faith has *some* vital and genial relation to it is certain. We read the very phrase (Acts xv. 9) in St. Peter's address to the earliest of all Church Councils. He speaks there of the impartial grace which has blest alike Jewish and Gentile disciples, and his words are that in both alike God has "purified their hearts by Faith." That is to say that, in some wonderful way, whatever the way in the last analysis might be, heart-purity had been realized in these converts through personal trust in a Person.

Can we give ourselves any account of this work of Faith in the purification of the will, and watch it, as it were, in the act of effecting the Christian's victory over sin within him? To travel at once to the heart of the matter, we approach an answer when we say that Faith is essentially "the Christ-receiving grace." Faith, as we saw when we examined its relation to our forgiveness and acceptance, is a hand capacious because empty, opened and extended to receive the gift unspeakable, the Son of God. And He is not only our peace, our pardon. In His divine union with our being, as He mysteriously but really penetrates us with His indwelling presence, He is our power, our victory, our purity. Thus the Faith which receives the Christ of God receives into the believer the virtues of His Life as well as endows him with the merits of His Passion.

The principle of spiritual victory through Faith is largely illustrated and exemplified in the Bible. The student of the Psalms, in quest of their deep and manifold messages to the soul in conflict, must often be struck with this. "Through God we shall do valiantly, for He it is that shall tread down our enemies" (Psalm cviii. 13); that utterance is a watchword which stands connected not only with a long chain of Psalm texts but with the whole spirit of the Psalmists as they think of their enemies and of their God.

The eleventh chapter of the Hebrews (of which more elsewhere) deals indeed mainly with the victories of Faith in the sphere of external difficulty. But it also shows us an Enoch who, through Faith, "walked with God"; that is to say, as the Greek version of Genesis paraphrases and expounds the Hebrew, "pleased God." And, when it sums up the achievements of the old saints in their life of Faith, we read that they not only stopped the lion's mouth and turned to flight the aliens on the stricken field, but "obtained promises" and "wrought righteousness" by Faith. Through Faith they were such that "of them the world was not worthy."

We further examine the New Testament, and we find the same deep principle greatly developed there. We have seen what St. Peter said about it at Jerusalem. Years afterwards, in his First Epistle, he carries out the thought. The Christian is "kept by the power of God, through Faith," till he receives the final "salvation" of heaven

(1 Pet. i. 5). He resists the devil, "steadfast by his Faith" (v. 9); kept true by trust in the living Christ.

St. John affirms that the spiritual victory of the new-born disciple over "the world" is by Faith (1 John v. 4). St. Paul discloses his own inmost secret of the victorious life, and it is the same: "The life which I live in the flesh," that is to say, under the circumstances of mortality, with all their snares and burthens, "I live by Faith in the Son of God" (Gal. ii. 20). In one transcendent passage (Eph. iii. 14–19), where he recounts to the disciples the themes of his own ardent intercession for them, it is just this which is his central thought: "I bow my knees to the Father, that you may be strengthened by the Spirit, that Christ may dwell," may come into settled residence, *κατοικῆσαι*, "in your hearts, *by Faith*."

Here we touch the vital centre of the truth. The heart where "Christ dwells" is, so far as His residence there is unhindered and entire, the purified heart. Let Him be welcomed not into its vestibule only but into its interior chambers, and the Presence will itself be purity. Before Him so coming, so abiding, the strife of passion cannot but subside. Flowing out from His intimate converse there, the very love of God will mix itself with the motives and the movements of the will. The heart thus made the chamber of His life will by a sure law reflect His character; nay, it will find itself shaped and dilated by His heart, not from its exterior or circumference, but from its centre.

The picture of the apocalyptic Epistle (Rev. iii. 20) will be interpreted in all its secret beauty in such an experience: "If a man hear My voice and open the door,

I will come in to him, and will sup with him, and he with Me." And what is the "opening of the door"? St Paul here annotates the Revelation: Christ comes to "dwell in the heart—*by Faith*." The trust which takes Him at His word, which fears not to let Him in, with all His will, with all His authority, welcoming Him to be indeed the Master in His own house, this it is which is the opening of the door. To this precisely He responds by "coming in" to be not peace only but purity for sinful man.

Has not the experience of innumerable Christians, in all the generations, affirmed the reality of this wonderful thing? Again and again it has been found that, when a thousand efforts in man's own name have failed really to conquer some bosom sin, the trustful invocation of the present Christ has brought sudden and surprising victory, mysterious but a fact.

The restless temper, the inveterate bad habit of life, the unholy play of imagination, the moral cowardice towards duty or suffering—they have yielded to a power not of us, yet deep within us, when we have remembered our Indweller and "lived by Faith in the Son of God." "I used in my youth," said a friend of mine, "to find one talisman always victorious against the tremendous temptations of the flesh and the devil. It was simple, but all-powerful. With shut eyes, solemnly, I said to myself the potent words, 'JESUS CHRIST.'"

That was the voice of Faith. The man knew that the victory lay only there, and, trusting, he cast all upon his Lord.

"What is it," said another true teacher in my hearing, "what is it in practical experience to 'live by Faith in the Son of God'? It is to conquer temptation by *making use of Him* as victory and law."

Let us not hope, or fear, that such "holiness by Faith" means an effortless and easy life. Every day and every hour the will must be alert and working if, at the centre of the soul, we are to maintain the contact with God which Faith effects. The soul indolent, the soul asleep, can never "live by Faith." We must *will* to explore the Bible, both for precept and for promise. We must *will* to pray, and evermore to pray. We must, like Mr. Standfast in the *Pilgrim's Progress,* determine to be often on our knees on the dark Enchanted Ground. We must *will* to use the sacramental means by which our contact with the Lord of the New Covenant is conveyed to us at once through the body and the soul. We must *will* to remember, as we take the holy Cup, that it "*is* the New

Covenant in His blood," and that the Covenant includes, as its greatest and final term, the transfiguration of the will.

But all these acts and works will be, not the substitutes for Faith, but its divinely efficacious helps and guides. In the last analysis the disciple will live, and will overcome, everywhere and always, alike in the uplifting hour of worship and in the heavy day of secular toil, in the open field of life and in the inmost of its secrecies of trial, "by Faith in the Son of God," spirit to Spirit, "nothing between."

FAITH . . .
AND THE BIBLE

CHAPTER X

FAITH AND THE BIBLE

THE purpose of this chapter is strictly limited. The Holy Bible is a subject of enquiry incalculably large, inexhaustible in its variety and depth. Even to tabulate the main questions raised solely by its literary and historical phenomena would be a long and ponderous task. To discuss even in outline the growth and structure of the Bible, in any adequate degree whatever, would demand an elaborate volume. To enter upon the examination of its Inspiration is to approach a series of complex problems, some of them insoluble.

I propose to myself here a task humbler and more possible. I wish to state some considerations upon the Bible which for my own mind have contributed more or less to the assurance that this Book really is the oracle and authority to which Faith may safely go as to a "divine informant." Such a position it claims in many ways, direct and indirect. If the claim is good, it is in the highest degree, of course, important. Let me think again for myself, and as it were in the presence of my reader, whether it is good indeed.

The Bible then, as a book, lies before me here on my writing-table. This particular copy is sacred to me by association; it belonged once to a disciple of Christ deeply dear to me, and it bears marks throughout of its former owner's use of it as the oracle of her Lord, before her call came to pass upwards into His radiant presence. This simple fact is not only moving to my heart; it is useful to my mind. For it is one minute but sacred item of the vast history of the Bible, the *tradition* of it, the handing on of it within the Christian community as the Holy Book.

Such a tradition is historically and morally important. It is a weighty thing to know, on valid grounds, that this Book, precisely no more and no less than this, was recognized as the gift of God to the Church fully fifteen centuries ago; that the far larger part of it was thus recognized at a time so early in Christian history that the Apostles of Christ were then either living or a living memory, and that the first and larger of the two great sections of the Book, the Old Testament, practically as we have it, was reverenced and trusted by our Lord Himself.

No thoughtful man will contemplate lightly a volume with such a tradition, that is to say, transmitted through such a history. It will carry to him at least a *prima facie* claim to reverent attention.

Then next, as a thought in order, this reverent attention will discover, on the reading and examination of the Book itself, certain phenomena of unique impressiveness. This Book is a thing alone and apart in literature, viewed from within, viewed as it indicates to us its own construction. We find, almost at first sight, that it is one Book yet also many; that it is many books yet also one.

Its oneness is sufficiently attested, not so much by any definite authoritative *dictum* as by the verdict of time and of man. In all the Christian centuries, and now, within these recent times of world-wide translation and circulation, in all regions and races, the conscience and heart of man have found in the Bible a moral and spiritual unity, a oneness of pervading truth and tone, impossible fully to define, but impossible not to feel where there is any sympathy with the Bible at all. Further, this unity is a unity of growth. It speaks less of the work of collectors of a library who, finding a host of scattered volumes, have classed them as best they could, than of the achievement of the projector of a multifarious yet co-ordinated work, who directs and controls an army of writers through a long series of years till his ideal is attained.

In a recent perusal of the greater part of the Old Testament, book after book from the beginning, this impression has been deepened on my mind. I speak of the broad surface of the writings; to deal with details is impossible. But speaking so, I have felt, as if for the first time, that Genesis does not merely precede the later histories by an artificial arrangement, but is to them as the root is to the tree, or as the stem is to the branches. As I go forward, even to the latest Prophets, I find the same impression continuously deepened.

When I pass to the New Testament the impression becomes indefinitely deeper still. The whole wonderful dual volume is the progressive record of a vast development, historical and spiritual, from epoch to related epoch, from stage to stage of moral revelation and education, from the primeval to the perfect. It bears, even as Nature does, the mysterious impress of fore-ordering Mind. And all along, even from the first, that Mind lets itself be seen not only in the growth of events and the evolution of ages, nor even only in manifold intimations of the character, one and consistent, of Him whose mind it is, but in the recurrence ever and again of definite intimations of a great future, a coming Kingdom, a coming King, intimations altogether unlike vague inferences or happy guesses. Rather, a sublime "second sight," a foreseeing and foretelling beyond the faculties of humanity, runs through the whole texture of the Old Testament till it finds its magnificent fulfilment in the New.

When the Christ came, He came *expected*, as to race, and region, and date. In a hundred particulars, to be sure, He threw current expectations into great perplexity, and even put them to shame, by His moral and spiritual transcendence over them. But when He, and they, are compared with the prophecies, we find that the current expectations were only wrong in their failure to apprehend the sublime idea of the Prophets. The Jew was perfectly justified in his certainty that the Prophets had a superhuman foresight of a fulfilment in which, through

Israel, Judah, David, and at such a time, and within such a region, the Deliverer of man should come.

Yet all the while this mysterious unity of the Bible embraces a multiplicity which makes it more mysterious still. At the very lowest reckoning it is the work of sixty writers; under the narrowest limitations of a morbidly sceptical literary criticism, their activity (taking both Testaments into view) covers nine centuries. They were members of widely different classes, men of many callings, many characters, and so scattered in respect of date that no concert among them, however vague, as to the goal and issue of their work, is to be thought of as possible.

The phenomenon of the Bible, as on one side a Literature and on the other side a Book, is as if in England we should have a volume, the product of English minds, beginning with Cædmon, or with Alfred, and ending, let us say, with Wordsworth or with Tennyson, which should yet be recognizable as not only a Collection, embracing elements of poetical and prose narrative, devotion, morals, and what not, each element carrying its own colour of character and of time, but also as a Work, full of inner unities, portable and usable as the ordered product of a presiding thought.

We have all this literary mystery in the Bible. And we have along with it, and in harmony with it, the manifestly superhuman, in the contents as well as in the structure. I do not here refer to the miracles, in the common meaning of that word. Not that I am sceptical of their reality, while fully conscious of the difficulties of such belief. I see them as phenomena not isolated but related, an avenue of wonder explained and justified only, but sufficiently, by the Temple to which it ascends—the culminating and supreme wonder of Christ, incarnate, sacrificed and risen. But I refer now rather to that phenomenon of *predictive* deeds and words of which we have already thought—prediction as little to be denied *a priori* as the verifiable phenomenon of the "second sight" in, for example, the Scottish Highlands, can be so denied. I refer also to that mystery with which the Book opens its first page, the song or vision of Creation. That page assuredly is not to be read as an account of origins given from the view-point of natural science. It is as little "literal" about the past, I take it, as the last chapters of the Revelation are necessarily "literal" about the future. But is it not a sign of the presence in that page of the superhuman that it, written at the very least (again I assume, for argument, a limit vastly too narrow, if I understand the case at all) more than two long millenniums ago, should be capable of discussion by expert students of nature within our own day * as an account of the preparation of earth for man, and of man for his true life, answering with substantial verity to the "testimony of the rocks"? What other primitive cosmogony could for half an hour sustain such a comparison?

Then I turn, in these reflections upon the Faith which I may lawfully use in listening to the Bible, to another range of witness. It is that of our Lord Jesus Christ. To Him, as the Gospels portray Him, the Old Scriptures were the word and oracle of His Father. They were this as much after as before His resurrection: a consideration which seems to me enough to dispose of the suggestion that His estimate of them was so

* See, *e.g.*, J. W. Dawson's *Modern Science in Bible Lands.*

conditioned by the limitations of His mortality that it was, in fact, only the reflection of the common beliefs around Him.

To Him personally the Scriptures were a divine guide and strength in His Temptation, in His Agony, on His Cross. They were equally His theme of discourse as He walked and talked (Luke xxiv.) with His followers after His supreme triumph over death. He manifestly left to His Church, as a perpetual legacy, His profound confidence in the Scriptures. And from within His Church, guided by His Spirit, there issued, within two brief generations of human life, a second Scriptural volume, holy writings which assuredly are *a fortiori* full of God and of His authority if what the Psalmists and the Prophets wrote was full thereof.

The Christ laid His hand in authentication upon the Old Testament. The

Christ, by His Spirit, so moved His Apostles and evangelical Prophets that they produced the New Testament. He stands before our Faith holding the two volumes, and clasping them into one. He witnesses to them, and He passes them over to us that they may witness to Him, as we open them under the light of His promised Spirit.

It is almost needless to explain at length why legitimately we use this witness of Christ to the Bible while yet it is only through the Bible, practically speaking, that we have historical knowledge of Christ. At first sight the argument may seem to run in a circle and so to be logically null and void. But it is not so, as a brief statement may remind us.

The Biblical portrait of Christ, to be recognized as historical, demands no antecedent theory of the inspiration of the record which presents it. It is properly self-evidencing; and thus. The Gospels, certainly the first three Gospels, were written not by men of imaginative genius. The first two Gospels indicate the possession by their compilers of the narrative faculty, and no more. The third Gospel shews a writer remarkable for sober care, but with no suggestion whatever of the creative instinct.

The fourth Gospel presents to us a writer who indeed can see far into both heights and depths. Yet we may safely say that he too, from the literary side, is *artless*. And from the spiritual side, does not his whole work bespeak the man who has *seen and worshipped?* He is possessed by the Personage with whom he deals; he is not speculating about Him. That Personage has found out his own inmost being, for adoration, and for a love inexpressible. His very depth of thought and word is a witness to the infinitely greater depth of his Theme, of the Christ for whose name and message he exists and of whose minutest acts he writes with a simplicity and detail unsurpassed, if it is even equalled, in the other Gospels.

Yes, the portrait of the Christ in the Gospels is self-evidencing. The character of the limners is such, as seen in their work, that we are reasonably sure that they could not have devised it or developed it. Therefore they saw it. Before them, historically, lived and moved, taught and worked, the Lord Jesus Christ, in *at least* all the grace and glory shewn in their picture of Him. They knew Him, they reported Him, in His visible, tangible, tender, benignant, yet always transcendent, reality.

Thus we are justified in taking as fact every essential element at least, of that picture. And assuredly one essential element is the attitude of the Christ of God towards the Scriptures. This was, this is, a living element of Himself.

Such, in outline, are some of the reflections with which I approach my Bible, and say to myself that this Book has for my Faith an authority which nothing else can have, as the articulate message of God to my soul from outside, from above. I consider its internal witness to itself. I consider the witness to it of the Christ, who is His own supreme evidence. And I approach it, so far as in reverence I can do so, as He approached it, asking, as a personal question of profound spiritual moment, "How read I? What is written?" And I ask this with the remembrance that He, by His Spirit, is able and willing—as assuredly He is needed—to "open my understanding, to understand the Scriptures."

I have said nothing upon the problem of the relation between the Bible and the Church, in regard to the guidance of the Faith of the individual, All that I would remark upon it, in view of our special line of reflection here, may be very briefly said. The current maxim which tells us that "the Church is to teach and the Bible to prove," is largely but not wholly sound. Certainly the Church has a vastly important teaching function; the most conspicuous example of its work in that field is the "Nicene" Creed; and what thoughtful Christian would give anything but an attention most reverent and humble to that great didactic voice of Christendom? No mind not altogether careless and self-confident would ignore the affirmations concerning revealed truth collected, embodied there. No, nor would any chastened mind refuse a reverential attention to guidance given by the Christian Communion in less primary vehicles of utterances; to the Articles, for example, if the man is an Anglican. To slight the great collective voices of the past is no good omen for the mind's security in the present and progress for the future.

But then other and balancing considerations have also to be remembered. The Church, however defined, is not a co-ordinate oracle beside the Bible. Still less is the Church a teacher such that the Bible is as it were its attendant, following it everywhere with "proofs" dutifully furnished to teachings assumed to be always correct. History shows the Church, the Jewish Church in our Lord's time and the Christian Church since then, greatly needing now and again to have its teaching not proved but corrected by the Bible.

The reverent Christian will reverence the Church. But he will also ask, reverently and on his knees, "How readest thou? What saith the Scripture?"

He will habituate himself to consult his Bible, remembering that its Author is beside him and can illuminate his spiritual study. And surely he, *if not a self-sufficient soul,* shall find the Bible, in the words of St. Athanasius, "self-sufficient for the declaration of the truth."

On purpose I have said not a word upon the numberless problems which Bible study presents in detail. I have not dwelt upon the great phenomenon of progressive revelation as shewn in Scripture, and the need with humility and prayer to interpret accordingly the earlier by the developed stages of that revelation. I have not called the reader to remember that this development implies in many things a moral advance from lower to higher; while yet the lower has its oracle-work still to do, taken in context with the higher and leading up to it. I have attempted no discussion of the problem of a supernatural accuracy of detail in Scripture; though for my own part I incline, after long years spent with the Bible, to err, if I may put it so, rather in that direction than in the opposite; only remembering that accuracy of narrative implies not necessarily a pedantic precision but report or record honourably adequate to its purpose.

These great questions however may be lawfully left aside by us just here. My one aim in this chapter is to indicate what may reassure the mind, as we open our Bible, that the Book is really God's great oracle for the guidance of our Faith in Him. And it is just in that opening of the Book, again and yet again, even to the end, that we shall find, if we know Christ, an unfailing renewal of our confidence in the pages which He so entirely trusted. "No defence of the Bible was ever written as effective as the Bible itself." We shall find that saying true, if the mysterious Book be not merely talked about, or casually turned over, but "read, marked, learnt, and inwardly digested."

To many a troubled mind, vexed with discussions carried on just outside the doors of the Bible, if I may put it so, there has come a great calm, and a great confidence, when once it has passed through the door into the dwelling. Let us keep company with the Bible, let us converse with it, let us make it our friend, and we shall get to find in it, by the grace of God, our light where all else is darkness, our guide where all else is bewilderment, and this even unto death. We shall fear no dishonouring of its promises, no disappointment of its hopes; no disenchantment of its principles of truth and love, no "other somewhat" instead of its Christ of God, when we pass at length beyond the veil into the light invisible.

FAITH . . .
AND SACRAMENTS

CHAPTER XI

FAITH AND SACRAMENTS

In a way as simple as possible let us think a little about the relation to Faith of those two great institutions of our Lord, the Sacrament of Holy Baptism and the Sacrament of Holy Communion.

Let not the reader anticipate a controversial discussion. It is too true that in the history of the Church the sacramental subject has been an occasion of many controversies. For more than a thousand years the mystery of the Holy Communion has been debated among Christians, sometimes with painful bitterness and anger. And the sister Sacrament has presented matter for anxious discussion, and sometimes for vehement antagonisms of opinion. Even the number of the rites and ordinances which are entitled to the name Sacrament has gathered around it a ponderous history of discussions.

But these troubled sides of a great subject will not much trouble us here. As to the numerical question, I explain at once that it is of Baptism and the Eucharist only that I treat. Following the twenty-seventh Anglican Article, I take these, and these alone, to be "Sacraments of the Gospel." The question whether other ordinances, not properly of "the Gospel," can be designated Sacraments, need not even be touched by me. And in our thoughts upon the two divine institutions which are Sacraments beyond a doubt, we shall consider them not from many points of view but from only one, namely their relation to Faith, to our personal trust in our personal Lord. This will give ample and peaceful matter for our thoughts.

"What meanest thou by this word Sacrament?" So the young disciple is asked in the English Catechism. Before we recall his answer, we will pause a moment to remember, in a general way, how the word Sacrament, *Sacramentum*, comes to be used in this particular connexion at all. It is not a Biblical word; at least, it nowhere occurs in our Authorized and Revised Versons.* Wide in its reference in Latin, so wide as to include the "sacred" military oath and any "sacred" subject of meditation, any "mystery" for devout thought, it was narrowed in the lapse of time to

* In the Latin Bible it is used to render the Greek word μυστήριον, for example in Eph. v. 32: "this is a great mystery." But there, and elsewhere in the ancient Latin versions, it appears to be used only in the large sense of *a sacred matter* of thought or action, not in any sense more limited and technical.

denote, in the Church, *rites* of special dignity and sanctity, and ultimately those which could claim our Lord's own institution.

Such rites, standing on a level of their own, manifestly invited the use of a special designation, and we welcome the word Sacrament as such. It has no Scriptural origin, but it is a suitable and now an immemorial specific term for ordinances of the highest possible Scriptural authority.

Taking the word as thus limited by the usage of ages, the Catechism bids the catechist ask his pupil what it means. And the pupil is to reply: "I mean an outward and visible sign of an inward and spiritual grace, given unto us, ordained by Christ Himself, as a means whereby we receive the same and a pledge to assure us thereof." Here the thoughts specially enforced are that the Sacrament, the Baptismal rite, the Eucharistic rite, is outward and visible, a thing which touches and affects the common senses, and can serve therefore as a "sign" recognizable by them, and then that it stands related to something "inward and spiritual," belonging to the region of the "inner man" and to the unseen and eternal life, which something is the grace of God, His free saving action and virtue for us and in us.

Further, this "sign" is what it is by virtue of the direct institution of our Lord, by whom it was "given," * "ordained," as nothing else of the outward and visible order was expressly sanctioned by Him.

Lastly, His sacred purpose in such gift and command is intimated. The "sign"

* There is evidence, for example in a Latin version of the Prayer Book published soon after the last Revision in 1662, that "given" as well as "ordained" belongs in this sentence to the word "sign."

is a means for the reception of the "grace," a channel by which our being finds contact with the spiritual action and virtue of God for our salvation. It is also "a pledge to assure us thereof," a token tangible and visible whereby we are to grasp with new certainty the fact of our possession, to be filled, as we contemplate the sign, with the animating conviction that this wonderful gift, the grace of God, is, for our future as well as for our present, "a sober certainty of waking bliss."

Are we tempted to think that our mental apprehension of it is a thing of evanescent emotions, a too partial inference from wish and hope? We are to consider the concrete, "outward, visible," sign of it. This will draw us out from all morbid misgivings into the strength and freedom of a certainty which God has sealed to the soul, through the body, on purpose that it may not be mistaken for a dream.

It is just this last aspect of the holy Sacraments to which I draw attention here. The whole passage quoted from the Catechism is a series of assertions closely linked together. To my own mind certainly there exists an intimate coherence between the idea of the sacramental rite as "means" and the idea of it as "pledge." The two words appear to me to throw light upon each other. They seem to indicate, for one point, that the word "means" here suggests the sort of channel which is illustrated, for example, by a royal deed of gift with its written terms, endorsed with the sign manual and seal, "*conveying*" to the right recipient the rightful possession of his promised title, office, property, or whatever it may be.

But this may here be left apart, for our immediate purpose. Enough to dwell awhile upon the relation which Baptism with its Water along with the Word, and the Eucharist with its Bread and its Wine along with the Word, bear to the Christian's Faith in the Christian's God. How do they tell upon that Faith as "pledges to assure us"? How, in the words of the noble Exhortation immediately before Communion provided in the Prayer Book, are they "pledges of the love of God, to our great and endless comfort"?

In reply, consider first the vital, the incalculable importance of the institution "by Christ Himself." Conceivably, the Church, in working out gradual processes of thought and action, might have instituted, prompted by human views of the fitting and the useful, a rite of initiation and a rite of continuing membership. But the Church was not left to do it. The Lord of the Church "gave and ordained" the ordinance of the holy Water, the ordinance of the holy Bread and Wine. As such, the Sacraments are not human things but divine. Their very first significance to us as we remember this is that in them God in Christ approaches man, touches man, speaks to man, by word and also by deed.

True, man also speaks in them to God. In Baptism the candidate is always understood to "yield himself unto God" in promises of loyalty and fidelity, and to ask from God gifts unspeakable—the adult by his own lips, the infant by proxy and in anticipation. In Communion, in the Eucharist, that is to say the Thanksgiving, the Christian is understood to remember, with a worshipping love, a love penitential while full of grateful joy, his crucified and atoning Lord, and to dedicate his being afresh in grateful surrender to His will and work. But these sides of the holy Ordinances are the secondary sides, not the primary, when we recall the fact that they were "ordained by Christ Himself." So viewed, their supreme value is that they speak to us from Him, before we use them as occasions in which we speak through them to Him.

In Holy Baptism, through the Water and the Word, we not only dedicated ourselves, personally or by deputy. We were assured by a divine act, as truly divine as if not only an Apostle but the Master Himself had plunged us in the water, or poured it on us as the representative equivalent to such immersion, that the dedication was accepted, the benediction given, the new life ours. I use words equally true and applicable in view of more than one theory of baptismal reception. It is true for those who understand the gift to be an infusion actual and immediate. It is true for those who take it to be done after the manner of deed and seal, awaiting its actualization when the recipient shall put in his claim—at that moment or later, as the case may be.

Under either type of doctrine, the tender and mighty message of the divine institution comes alike to our spirits. Here is the very "promise which He hath promised us, even eternal life" (1 John ii. 25), cast into concrete form, outward and visible. Here, embodied in a concrete action, is that new Birth, of which it is written (1 John v. 1) that "whosoever believeth that Jesus is the Christ is born of God." The Sacrament is as if in it God Himself bade His promise spring into a mode of existence visible and tangible; that through it we might almost see the Promiser Himself in act to give and bless, and that thus, to the utmost possible on this side the mortal veil, the struggle of Faith might transform itself into the rest of Faith, the tranquil certainty of spiritual sight.

Even so it is with the Holy Communion. If possible, it is even more so there. As far as I can see, neither Scripture nor the English Church intimates any difference *in kind* between the two divine Sacraments. But we may rightly think that the Eucharistic Feast is sacred *in a degree* of its own. Its indissoluble and soul-moving connexion with our Redeemer's supreme act of dying love, and His explicit bequest of it to be the ever-recurring joy and strength of our pilgrimage, even to the end, hallow it in a wonderful way to love and Faith.

Then let us approach it every time in order that we may in truth assure Him afresh that we are His. But first, and last, and most, let us come in order that He may afresh assure us in His own way that He is ours.

The supreme need of the Christian, as he travels up the slopes and steeps of life, is the spiritual sustenance of a living Christ, the Christ who, having died as his Sacrifice of peace, rose out of death, leaving death vanquished under His feet, to be his Life of power. To be sure of Him, Him given for us, Him living in us, as sure as spiritual certainty of the invisible can be made to us on earth, is the very life of our spirits, the food of their hunger, the strength of their weakness, their perpetual resurrection to a "newness of life" ever young—nay, ever younger, if youth means life in its genial growth and hope.

And He who "knoweth our frame," and how the physical and the spiritual play upon each other within us, has given us in the great Sacrament of His Body and His Blood His own all-gracious gift of precisely this more than "angel's food." Here we hold it, here we assimilate it, as actually ours; for us by Calvary, in us by Pentecost; Christ one with us, we one with Christ; our perfect secret for "peace with a holy God and power in an unholy world."

As I have said, there are great aspects of the Sacrament, and now particularly of the Sacrament of Thanksgiving, which I have not tried to touch upon here. I have kept strictly to that function of the holy rites which affects our Faith—Faith not in the Sacrament but in its Giver. But surely in this one view we shall find "riches unsearchable" as we approach, time after time, the festal Table of Redemption, Life, and Hope. Even in the purely mental region we shall recognize in the Holy Communion, on reflection, an "evidence of Christianity" of incalculable value. For nothing but the complete victory of the Lord over the grave could have made it possible that the Sacrament of *His Death* should be hailed by His followers as the Feast of thanksgiving and expectation. The existence, the persistence, of the Eucharist makes visible, as it were, the empty Sepulchre and the Risen One there beside it, as when He "turned to heaven the grief of Magdalene."

But behind the region of the intellect lies the region of conscience, of will, of love. And the disciple, as he takes the holy Bread broken before him, and the holy Wine poured out before him, is intended, invited, commanded, without a doubt, without a reserve—because he is taking and assimilating in his Master's own way his Master's pledge of the divine fulness of the gift of Himself—"to feed on HIM, in the heart, by Faith, with thanksgiving."

SOME DIFFICULTIES AND PROBLEMS

CHAPTER XII

SOME DIFFICULTIES AND PROBLEMS

THIS is a chapter of fragments. The great theme of Faith suggests to us, by the side as it were, a wide range of questions in detail, varying from high mysteries to matters of everyday life and duty. Here we will try to touch, and little more than touch, some of these.

But here let us well remember that the main duty of the Christian life is not to discuss, but to obey. When our feet have found, in any valid sense, the rock of Faith in God through Christ, we are then *to walk* upon that rock, from trial to trial, duty to duty, strength to strength. The shadows beside us and before us, however much they may demand

and engage our sight, are never to hinder our feet. And it is as our feet move forward, as we advance in the life of practical loyalty to a trusted God, that we shall be best preparing to see many of those shadows melt into light, and be best enabled to wait in patience till the perfect day shall dissipate them all for ever.

i. First, a few words in general about difficulties of Faith. It lies in the nature of the case that Faith should have difficulties. We saw in the opening pages of this book that the exercise of Faith implies a measure of the unknown around us. It occasions continually the question whether, in face of the unknown, antecedent to the clearing away of the unknown, we will trust. This is, of course, *a difficulty*, a something which calls for the effort of a venture, less or greater. Granted the whole ground known, and the way to traverse it quite visible, open, and feasible, the passenger has no need of Faith ; the word would be out of connexion with his experience. Difficulties, things which challenge trust and test it, are the necessary environment of Faith.

ii. This is fully true about mental as well as about practical difficulties of Faith. The life of Faith, as one aspect of the spiritual life, is surrounded with the mysterious, the unexplained, the unrevealed. In it we are asked to take our Lord at His word about many a sombre fold of the "clouds and darkness which are round about Him" (Psalm xcvii. 2). We may think till reason totters, yes, till it gives way, over the riddle of evil, over the relation of man's will to an eternal purpose, over the permanence of our personality, over personality itself, over the concurrence of personality and infinity in God. We may literally lose ourselves in meditation on the vastness of the material universe, on the ultimate nature of space and of time; we may think till we seem literally to sink into nothing amidst the illimitable spheres and æons. The one valid reassurance, when such trials seriously assail the reason, may be stated in an aphorism due, I think, to Richard Whately, and obviously true at every step in common life: "Never let what you know be disturbed by what you do not know."

A whole world of mental mystery may be lighted up, quite adequately for our peace and hope, by the Apostle's watchword, "I know Him whom I have believed," Him whom I have trusted. Do I know personally, spiritually, on solid grounds, outward and inward, Him who knows all, Him in whom all things, with the whole mystery of their relations, live, move, and have their being? To know

Him is to find, in many instances, the right point from which to get some insight into the unknown. But most certainly it is the warrant for precisely such repose about the unknown as shall liberate us to arise and serve Him in the path of duty. To have caught sight of the living God is to be able to trust Him with everything.

iii. The same truth holds, of course, amidst the practical mysteries of life regarded in relation to Faith. Take the frequent and often most distressing mystery of apparently fruitless prayer. That is a riddle which haunts earnest souls far more widely and far more painfully than many of us know. What occasions its peculiar weight, for the reverent Christian, is the decision and emphasis of our Lord's precepts and promises about prayer. Some of these, taken in the letter, would seem to justify the expectation that literally anything, including great physical miracles, is normally feasible, accessible, in answer to the prayer of Faith.

But we look around, or we look within, and facts appear to be far from correspondent with such words. I do not wish to minimize the pain of the phenomenon; who could possibly do so who has once felt it? But here also I recur to Whately's principle; never to let our hold upon the really known be disturbed by the unknown.

Is God in Christ indeed known to us? Nay, to put the question with more reserve, Are we reasonably assured that the Christ of the Gospels, as we thought of Him in an earlier chapter,* is the supreme historical and spiritual reality? Then let us set that assurance up in fullest view amidst all other thoughts.

* See p. 175.

Those thoughts will get from it a patience and an illumination which will at least relieve the pain, and may suggest the path towards great solutions hereafter. We shall be reminded, for one thing, that, till we know as much as He does, we are imperfect judges of what is and what is not fruitless prayer.

Certainly we can never, as we are, judge perfectly whether such and such a prayer will finally prove to have been fruitless. We shall recollect also that prayer deals not with a mere law of effect and cause but with a Person, infinite in resource, supreme in kindness, and also sovereignly free as to His all-wise volitions how to meet each case of supplication.

Can we ever dictate to such a Listener how He shall reply, and when? To be sure of Him is to be sure of an infallible and benignant attention. But it is to speak in a Presence where we must not only ask but trust. For the speech is to a Personality, free amidst the boundless variety of conditions, free to keep silence or break it, to move visibly or be still, not capriciously, yet with personal choice, wholly seeing the whole case.

So knowing Him, we shall bear, with a submission not in the least fatalistic, but full of trust, His silences as well as His replies. He listens, He loves, He is true. And we have not yet (James v. 11) "seen the end of the Lord." Moses prayed to enter Canaan, and was refused —this side the grave. But he stood on the Mount of Transfiguration, with his Lord, in glory—another day.

iv. Or take the perplexities of "Providence." They are as painful as possible to those who observe without believing. It has been said that Faith finds more trials in the stories of crime and disaster in one daily newspaper, or in one walk through the slums of London, than in the whole Bible with all its problems of critical interpretation.

We stand silent and distressed before the "Providence" which permits the daily record of wreck, fire, famine, to roll on, the mine to overwhelm its workers, the train to quit the rails in a leap of death, the earthquake to massacre a population; while with a more normal and persistent activity, in forms indefinitely worse, for they blend moral with material evil, the work of sin goes forward in murder, fraud, oppression, falsehood, enmity, private, social, national, —a scene of evil wide as mankind.

When reason has done what it can to reduce, as it were, the phenomenon, and even when the observer is doing what he can in practice to abate it within his little sphere, it still forms a tremendous trial and a manifold one. It involves, for one element, the pain of the loyal heart, a pain well known to the Prophets, as it sees its Lord mistaken and blasphemed, or at best regarded as a Being apart and negligible amidst the sorrow and the wrong over which He keeps such long silence. What can we do at such moments but fall back upon *what we know?* We know HIM—not anyhow, but in Christ, the Christ who, coming from the central secret of existence, proved Himself, in an immeasurable self-sacrifice, to be Love the gift of Love. Knowing Him so, and not yet knowing His "end," we can trust. Trusting, we can both bear and work. It is a victory of Faith.

I possess a treasure private and my own. It is a book-marker, in which a hand long buried, a hand most dear to me, has worked in blue silk a text upon a pierced card. The "wrong" side is apparently nothing but a tangle of unintelligible confusion. The "right" side shows, in faultless lettering, the unfathomable words, "GOD IS LOVE." I once held up that card to a great congregation of workpeople in a "pit-village," just after a shocking disaster underground which had desolated a score of homes. It seemed to hush and to uplift the troubled host of listeners, who were in no mood for conventional consolation. It was a pregnant parable—and not for them only. Faith can anticipate, and await, the turning of the pierced card of life over to its right side at last.

v. A few words may be said here on the subject of Faith and bodily healing. This is a matter widely present in current religious thought. I speak of it as it is debated in strictly Christian circles. This is not the place, I think, for passing over the borders of the Church to comment at length upon what is termed Christian Science. If I understand aright, the beliefs covered by that somewhat inclusive term do not, and cannot, claim to be Christian in the common import of the word, that is to say, to be based on the Person and teaching of the incarnate, crucified, risen Christ of the Bible and the Creeds. And if I read the central tenets of Christian Science aright, its claim to deal with pain and sickness by immaterial means is not properly the claim of Faith. Rather, to use the terminology of ancient controversies of the "Gnostic" period, it is a claim for the remedial power not of *pistis,* but of *gnôsis.* It appeals to a mysterious *knowledge* that matter, and with it physical pain, are illusions, rather than to a *trust* reposed in a living Promiser, transcendent, present, holy, loving, who can win victories for us over material evil.

Here I speak rather of the conviction of a great and growing number of earnest Christians that Faith has a great work to do for bodily healing as truly as for spiritual, and that this work is so seldom done because the Christian Church has had too little Faith in our Lord's promises about it. It is pointed out that in His own practice He was everywhere Healer as well as Teacher, and that He constantly connected Faith with the healing process, particularly Faith exercised by the patient towards Himself. Then, He commissioned His Apostles to be healers as well as teachers, and so in fact they were. Among the pentecostal "gifts" Healing was expressly included. Not all disciples when filled by the Spirit possessed it, but many did, as others possessed (1 Cor. xii. 8–10) the gift of prophecy, or of tongues.

We are reminded that St. James

(v. 14, 15) indicates that in his day, along with a religious act of anointing by the presbyters, "the prayer of Faith" was efficacious to "save the sick," to effect recovery. Why is this no longer the recognized belief and practice of the Church? "Is the Lord's arm shortened? Is His ear heavy?"

Here first let it be said that in all such appeals there is a large and weighty element of truth. To speak of the matter for the moment from the side of "nature," it is quite true that thought, especially in the form of will, has a mysterious but real potency upon matter, and can and does thus work wonders upon weakness and pain, even when God is not invoked. Then beyond doubt the experience of Christendom bears witness, more or less in all ages, not least in our own, to the fact that prayer can and does win healing and health in ways which only a prejudiced scepticism can deny.

To myself one such example is personally known where all the essential conditions were such as to assure sober reason that, where science had altogether failed, "the prayer of Faith" (accompanied in that case with a solemn unction) succeeded. I not only admit, I earnestly affirm, that we are called to use the power of Faith in a direct and particular appeal to the Lord of life, simply relying on His will and power, for the arrest and healing of bodily disease, very much more than we have done hitherto, taking the Church as a whole. It is quite possible that we are being led in the wisdom of God to aim at larger victories in this direction, precisely at a period of formidable doubt and misgiving around and even within the Church.

Only, this line of truth, this conviction that Faith is to "obtain promises" for the body, needs, like every other, the safeguard of co-ordinate truths, or it will soon be distorted into an error. One such truth is that the ills of the body, unlike those of the will, are not absolute evils in their own nature, though connected with man's fall. A sickness may be (John xi. 4) "for the glory of God." It may be the occasion for such an application of the discipline of pain as shall conspicuously result in the highest spiritual health. Accordingly, it cannot be so dealt with by Faith as if we knew infallibly, in the particular case, that the suffering is contrary to God's will.

Nor again is there any reason in Scripture for the opinion that the use of medical skill for healing is a contradiction to Faith, and as such a dishonour to the power of God. The Bible abounds with illustrations of the practical harmony between the truest reliance on the divine will and power and the sober use of the means which are, as we look at their ultimate nature, part of the providential equipment of man by his Creator and Preserver. The truth that "man liveth by every word that proceedeth out of the mouth of God" (Matt. iv. 4) does indeed amply prove, as our Lord took it to prove, that man's bodily life can be sustained by spiritual forces only, if God wills it. But it does not prove that the use of food is a contradiction to Faith in the common order of life.

Briefly, to sum the matter up, there lie resources for our bodily frame, great and precious, in Faith and in the prayer of Faith. A wise and reverent balance of thought is demanded as we think of them and use them. We are not to class bodily evil with spiritual, so as to place the relief of the body on the same plane of Christian blessing with the salvation of the soul. We are not to confuse the fulness of Faith with the neglect of means. But we are to seek in this, as in other regions of our complex life, a large growth of Faith even into greatness. And here, as in all things, we are to remember that great Faith means not greatness in our mental or spiritual action, but a clear, a single-hearted, view of the glorious greatness of the Object of Faith, and therefore a great simplicity of trust in Him.

THE CLOUD .
OF WITNESSES

CHAPTER XIII

THE CLOUD OF WITNESSES

It is an inspiring thought with which the twelfth chapter of the Hebrews opens. A picture rises before the holy Writer, vast and vivid, and he transmits it to his readers. The runners of the Greek *stadium* suggest it, and the multitudinous spectators who, from the seats which overlooked the course, tier rising above tier, watched the race and its victories. We mortal Christians, living by Faith, are the runners. Our immortal forerunners, looking from their heavenly rest, are the spectators of our conduct and our course.

The picture takes us back to the eleventh chapter of the Epistle. There we, in our turn, though after a far different fashion, occupy the place of observation, while before us pass the ancient saints, running the race that was set before them. In a long and glorious file we watch them hastening to the goal, patient, persistent, overcoming, all "obtaining a good report through Faith." The enumeration is inspired. It is a selection, "caused to be written for our learning." Let us close our thoughts upon Faith by some simple reflections upon the work of Faith as we see it in the men of the eleventh chapter of the Epistle to the Hebrews.

In earlier pages* we referred to this great Biblical discourse, we may almost call it this great Biblical poem, upon Faith. We found that it begins with words which are not a definition of Faith in itself but rather a description of Faith at its work, an account of its potency

* See pp. 27, 153.

to make things hoped for concrete and tangible and things unseen as certain as if evinced by reasoned proofs. The long procession of the children of Faith which follows is to be studied with that initial text in view; our own running of the race of Faith is to be the better for the study.

The quoted examples of believing begin, somewhat paradoxically, with our own recognition by Faith of the superhuman origin of the universe and its order and development. "Through Faith we understand that the æons," the ages, so literally, "have been constituted by the Word of God." In order to take his departure from the first pages of the Bible, the Writer thus first reminds us that our certainty of a divine Free Will, willing the finite into being, is in the strictest sense an issue of Faith. Now and for ever the origin of things is unseen, inscrutable. But we know it, we "understand" it, to be divine. For the God who, in ways untold, has proved to us His veracity, has informed us, in His Word, that so it was. We touch the unseen past, as we clasp the unseen future, by trust in a trustworthy Person, that is to say, by Faith.

Then begins the procession of the Faithful of old. Its significance stands perfectly clear of merely chronological problems. To date at all narrowly the advent of man upon the earth is now widely felt to be as impossible as to explain by a sheer literalism the story of his creation. That story is no mere myth, nor mere parable; it is history—but history given us in hieroglyphic. Yet the human persons here named, the Abel of this passage, and the Enoch, and the Noah, are none the less real (as real assuredly they were to the incarnate Lord) for all the mystery of their surroundings. Their humanity was ours. Their hearts, their wills, even as ours, felt moral trial, and knew perplexity of thought, and could not reach by sight into the unseen.

So Abel is our example, approaching God in a way (this is evidently implied) prescribed through some primeval oracle from above, and followed with the obedience of a trusting soul. So Enoch "walked with God," "pleased God," in a life which was carried up at last unbroken into immortality, but which (this is evidently implied) was one long practical reliance upon testimony, outward and inward, concerning an unseen Person, supreme, adorable, lovable, trustworthy. So Noah in his turn "walked with God" (Gen. vi. 9), and saw and touched the unseen future, by Faith, by trust in the Person who told him of the coming ruin and of the way of safety. Noah's example stands alone of its kind in the chapter, and full of a profound significance. His was Faith towards God in His merciful warnings, just and awful. Let us follow him, and fear, and trust.

Then passes before us "the father of the Faithful" with his company—Sarah, Isaac, Jacob, Joseph; Amram and his wife, and their wonderful son; judges, kings, prophets; mourners and martyrs of Israel, early and late, famous and nameless. They represent experiences of every variety. Here is the Friend of God himself, leaving the Chaldean city for that long nomadic life to which he was not born, "taking up permanent residence in tents," * because of reliance upon a promise which did not even localize its prospect.

Here Sarah finds that generosity of

* Ἐν σκηναῖς κατοικήσας (Hebrews xi. 9).

recognition which sometimes surprises us in Scripture, God's praise for *latent* grace and truth. Her motherhood was conditioned by her believing the impossible. It was granted because, after that first incredulous laughter (Gen. xviii. 12) she "counted Him faithful that had promised."

Then Faith overcomes its most tremendous trial, when the child of the Promise is laid by his father on the altar. And then again comes in the gracious paradox, the unexpected praise; old Isaac's submission to the Will he had resisted, his sudden accent of energy, "yea, and he shall be blessed" (Gen. xxvii. 33), classes him too with the conquerors and seers by Faith.

Jacob on his death-bed believes, obeys, and worships, passing on the tribal blessing in God's, not nature's, order. And Joseph, the old illustrious minister of imperial Egypt, clasps by Faith to his dying heart the promise of Canaan, and casts his lot in with it, claiming there his grave of hope.

At the very darkest hour of the chosen line the parents of Moses, because of that promise, save the glorious infant which is hereafter to serve in effecting its fulfilment. And he, in his time, with a Faith all the more wonderful because Providence itself might have seemed to a less clear eye to have given him Egypt for his inheritance, and to have trained him for it, " forsakes " it. He " sees the Invisible One " in His promise, and so he does the will of God, step by step, in the great Exodus, not in its wonder-works only but in that pilgrim-meal and that sprinkling of the blood which were to break every alien tie, while they assured, to Faith and only Faith, a heavenly shelter. So the host of delivered bondsmen traversed the parted sea, they too sharing, in some sudden victorious exaltation, their leader's Faith. And so their sons, finding evidence enough of things hoped for in the promise and presence of their God, compassed the walls of Jericho till they fell.

Then again follows one of the paradoxes of the Bible. The sinful pagan woman has her name written next in the pedigree of Faith. We could not have done it, but the inspiring Spirit, to whom all hearts are open, can. He finds in Rahab one who took at His word the God of Israel, just and pure, and hailed Him for her God, and saw the coming victory of His cause as if it were already won. Here and by St. James (ii. 25) her name is honoured. She stands inscribed (Matt. i. 5) among the ancestors of the Christ Himself.

She, wonderfully, is the last name inscribed with detail upon this roll of honour. Then, in groups and throngs, we see pass by the men and the women of Faith born in the later days. Here pass the warriors of the "iron age," who, against all appearances of hope, but trusting the God of Israel, turned the aliens to flight in their hour of tyrannic pride. Here is Samuel, the second Moses, believing and obeying amidst a cataclysm of invasion, and thus enabled to build the ruins up. Here is David, made patient by Faith under the trials of his heroic youth, and, not less wonderfully, believing still, and serving still, in the power of Faith, after his own sin had wrecked his gladness. The Prophets are here, whose Faith showed best its superhuman source in God when, age after age, they foretold most confidently the coming King just when Israel most shamefully failed, and most sorrowfully fell, and Assyria and Chaldea had their way and will.

And the joy of the stricken mothers at Zarephath and Shunem is not forgotten, claiming life out of death for their sons because "against hope they trusted in hope." And the confessors and martyrs of the Old Covenant have their memorial, from Elijah in the desert, believing again after his despair, to the "children" in the Chaldean furnace, and the Maccabean victims of the latest time.

It is a majestic roll and record. The holy Chronicler casts over it all, under his Inspirer's spell, a light spiritual and eternal. He bids us know that Abraham and his sons had insight and foresight which transcended Canaan, and found a limit only in the heavenly country and the city out of sight. He tells us that Moses grasped enough of the great Hope of man through Israel and Messiah to make Israel's "reproach" glorious to him as "the reproach of Christ." And the martyrs met their cruel deaths with the thought of "a better resurrection," even to eternal life.

So passes the line along, to blessed rest, to the sight which follows Faith. And then, supreme and alone, yet in a mysterious fellowship, there walks before us (xii. 2), till He is seen ascending to the throne above, the all-perfect Exemplar, the "Prince and Accomplisher * of our faith," JESUS, the absolute Believer; JESUS, that "better Thing" for which the fathers looked, and which we now behold and possess. To Him, in His holy humanity, Faith was an experience as genuine as it is for His disciples. Resting upon His Father's word, not upon sight nor upon sensation, but upon that word, He looked for the immeasurable "joy set before Him." By that Faith, not by the aids of His Deity but by that perfect human

* ἀρχηγὸν καὶ τελειωτήν.

Faith in the Promise, He endured, He issued victorious out of the unfathomable Passion.

It is needless, as we close our brief and fragmentary meditations, to draw out at length the message, the *envoi*, of the eleventh chapter of the Hebrews, crowned by this climax in the twelfth. Let it only and simply be remembered that the great *stadium* of the race of Faith has never been empty of runners to this hour, and that never were the unseen ranks of the witnesses of the course, that "long cloud" of which the great hymn * sings, so multitudinously full as they are at this day. Nor let it be forgotten how St. Paul bids us recollect that another and all-radiant cloud hovers watching over us. Read Eph. iii. 10, and see how "the principalities and

* "Give me the wings of Faith."

the powers in the heavenly places" look upon the Church, upon "the blessed company of all *Faith-ful* people," with eyes which seek to read in its life and victories "the manifold wisdom" of their God.

In the power of Faith to make certain the hoped for and the unseen visible to souls "burthened with the flesh," and beset as they go by the devil and the world, the heavenly Watchers see a wonder which their sublime point of observation displays to them as more wonderful than we can guess, revealing to them depths and lights in the eternal wisdom which their own region, sinless and sorrowless, could not possibly have shewn. Let us remember the angelic "cloud of witnesses" also, as well as the human, and feel the inspiration of its attention as we go.

Yes, we also, by Faith, will "run with patience." Do our circumstances seem too prosaically modern for the exercise of a spiritual power lofty as that of the days of Abraham or of Isaiah? But it was always modern times. The seen and temporal always clung around the child of Faith; he was always also the child of his period, even as we are of ours. But his Deliverer was stronger than his circumstances, and Faith made him partaker of his Deliverer's power over them. He was, not in principle only, but in practice, according to his Faith, that is to say, according to his use of the resources of his trusted Lord, "delivered from this present evil world" (Gal. i. 4) as it existed around him then. His Deliverer, whose being is transcendent over time, is ours also now. For us to-day, even as in the remotest and the greatest past, the hand which appropriates Him and uses His power is nothing less nor more than Faith.

Is human hopefulness waning around

us in this burthened age? A trusted Christ is the unalterable warrant of the reality of "the blessed hope." Is the visible and tangible oppressively strong upon us? Does the "conquest of nature" seem only to involve us deeper in the bondage of a material ideal? A trusted Christ can burst that inner prison. We may live above even that tyranny "by Faith in the Son of God," for He is the immovable and victorious evidence of the things not seen, which are eternal. We still can live a life which is life indeed, to God, for man, in Love and Hope, through Faith.

www.ingramcontent.com/pod-product-compliance
Lightning Source LLC
LaVergne TN
LVHW050619100826
845148LV00011B/1654

9781556352546